DATE DUE

NOV 28 1983	FEB 10 1993	JUL 2 5 2005
JAN 3 1984	MAR 1 1993	SEP 1 2 2008
	DEC 2 0 1993	JUL 1 3 2010
FEB 14 1984	DEC 2 9 1994	OCT 0 6 2014
OCT 2 3 1984	MAR 1 5 1995	
MAR 8 1995	MAY 01 1995	
OCT 2 5 1986	AUG 2 4 1995	
APR 1 5 1988	FEB 5 2001	
APR 2 1989	AUG 0 8 2003	
OCT 5 1989	FEB 2 6 2001	
NOV 2 7 1989		
FEB 17 1990	FEB 1 2 2001	
MAR 1 0 1990		
APR 16 1991		
DEC 18 1991	MAR 1 3 2001	
	FEB 1 1 2002	

**make it
from
felt**

make it
from
felt

phyllis w. goldman

Thomas Y. Crowell Company
New York • Established 1834

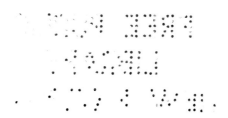

Designed by Jill Schwartz

Manufactured in the United States of America

L.C. Card 70-170994
ISBN 0-690-51144-2

1 2 3 4 5 6 7 8 9 10

2

For Bob
who cut out felt eyes, noses, and mouths for me,
and then cut out dangling participles for me—
my eternal gratitude. And for Josh and Matt, too.
   My thanks to Tom Bloom for his help with the
illustrations and patterns.

contents

introduction

One of the most rewarding accomplishments in life is to make something by hand. Whether that something is a pincushion sewn by a small child, a bookcase built by an older boy, or an afghan crocheted by a woman really doesn't matter. All have equal value because the child, the boy, and the woman can say proudly, "I made it myself."

This book tells you in simple, uncomplicated terms how you can make more than 50 felt items by yourself. And any one of them will cost you as little as 20 cents. A really expensive item shown in this book will run you a whopping 60 or 70 cents.

One Christmas a few years ago, I decided to make all the gifts I was going to give. With nothing but good intentions—I possessed no special talents—I sat down and designed my gifts. I created designs for pajama bags, beanbags, hand puppets, clipboards, key cases, pencil cases, and more. Then I went to the nearest notions shop to buy material to make my "originals." Suddenly, a pile of brightly colored pieces of felt caught my eye. The gay rainbow splash of the material had a festive air about it from the start. So I bought dozens of squares in a palette of colors, thread to match, some glue, bits of ribbon and yarn, and went home to start making my gifts.

My creations seemed to come to life after just a few minutes with a pair of scissors, a dab of glue, and a stitch of thread. Amazed at my own "talent"—I had never taken a course in art, design, sewing, or the like—I got carried away. I created more and more items and derived more and more pleasure from them. They were all a great success when presented to my friends and family and to my children and their friends. Perhaps the greatest satisfaction was making and giving these happy-looking gifts to the children in the pediatric ward at a nearby hospital. Their smiles were all the assurance I needed that my creations were a success.

That Christmas saw the start of a family hobby that still continues. I hope it will be a start for you, too.

So many people think they are "all thumbs" and can't do anything creative or original. Therefore, they never take up a satisfying or worthwhile hobby. Now the handling of power tools to build a dining-room table or the operation of a potter's wheel to mold a bowl may be beyond some people's mechanical aptitude or interest, but anyone who has ever cut out a paper doll or sewn a button on a dress can make all of the designs illustrated in this book. What's more, anyone, age six to sixty, can use my designs as a starting point from which to create his own designs.

The six-year-old at loose ends on a rainy day or confined to a sickbed with a cold will have hours of fun making bookmarks, eyeglass cases, pincushions, a change purse.

Elderly people will gain satisfaction from making clipboards for the local church fair or a wardrobe of dolls' dresses for grandchildren.

The woman who can snatch a few minutes or a few hours will find any or all of these projects rewarding.

The teen-ager with a limited allowance will discover that *making* a gift is often more appreciated than buying one.

Even men can get into the act by helping out with the pasting and cutting and even designing.

There is no end to the fun and satisfaction of making things out of felt, because felt possesses some amazing qualities.

First, the colors in which felt is available are more vivid and more varied than colors of almost any other material.

Second, it is easy to handle; it is flexible, durable, and it doesn't ravel.

And third, the cost is so small that great numbers of items can be made at a minimum expense.

As a matter of fact, you need no special tools, no special skills or talent, and no great output of time to see the fruits of your labor quickly. It's a hobby you can pick up or put down at any time of the day. A small box is all you'll need to store your materials.

There is no seasonal limit to the items you make. They are appropriate for gift-giving at Christmas, Easter, and birthdays. Felt novelties can be presented as baby gifts, house gifts, going-away gifts, party favors, and hospital remembrances. They can be made in large quantities for church bazaars, school fairs, hospital wards.

They can be made in individual activity or in group projects. As a group project, virtually any age can participate. For the child who is capable of using a pair of scissors, there is no safety hazard. Unlike certain other hobbies, work in felt requires no sharp tools, fire, heat, or electricity. The child can be left alone with hardly a possibility of danger.

The elderly person whose eyesight may be failing will find it easy to work with felt.

Although you shouldn't be sloppy about cutting or sewing,

working with felt does not require the precision that other materials—such as wood, plastic, metal, or clay—do. A wrong snip here or a half-inch off there can easily be corrected or adjusted.

This book has been divided into sections based on particular groupings of designs. The simplest designs are most appropriate for younger children. However, there is no age restriction or special skill level needed for *any* of the items shown in this book. Make the easy ones—make the slightly more ambitious ones—make them all. As you progress, you'll find yourself working with more confidence and imagination.

At this point you may be tempted by someone who looks at your professional results and says, "Why don't you go into business and *sell* these great-looking items?" In the last chapter of this book, I will give you dozens of reasons for *not* listening to that voice. I heard that very same voice once and lived (barely) to regret it. My advice is to make these designs for fun, for gifts, as a hobby during your spare time. Otherwise, it ceases being fun.

The designs here can be varied if you like. The colors suggested are merely the ones I use. If you don't think a mouse should be purple with red ears, cut him out in fuchsia and fawn-colored felt. And if you can't imagine a mushroom being red and white, make it plum and puce.

The next chapter contains hints and short cuts on making all of the items in this book. They are the results of my own trial-and-error experiences. I pass this information along to you for time-saving results. No doubt you'll think of others.

Whatever you do, whether you follow the designs to the letter or vary them a bit—the end result will be your own wonderful accomplishment. And there will come a day when someone asks you: "Where did you buy the clipboard next to your phone?" You will be able to answer: "I made it myself!"

1. hints to help

Before you rush out to buy anything, look around the house —in your sewing box, odds-and-ends box, even in your children's dresser drawers. You may already have more of the materials and tools needed than you think to make felt novelties.

First, you'll need a large pair of sharp scissors. The sharper the scissors, the easier it will be to cut through the layers of felt. If you must purchase the scissors, ask for an 8-inch dressmaker's light trimmer. However, if you already have a pair that is an inch shorter or longer, it will do fine.

You'll also need a small pair of sharp scissors for cutting the smaller and more delicate items. A good pair of embroidery scissors works very well.

Although pinking shears are not absolutely essential, they do enhance the look of some of the designs. Use pinking shears where indicated in the directions; otherwise, the dressmaker's straight trimmer will do. (Incidentally, a good way to sharpen scissors at home is to cut through rough sandpaper several timcs.)

Next, decide upon the colors you are going to use. Felt comes in literally hundreds of shades. Investigate your thread supply to see which matching colors you have on hand.

I find that a matching color is effective most of the time, but often a contrasting shade of thread in certain felt designs can provide a nice touch.

If you are planning to make large quantities of items in one particular color, you will find it cheaper to buy the large spool. A word of caution: at all costs, avoid nylon thread. It is very difficult to handle, whether sewing by hand or by machine.

Next, look for a good fabric glue. You might even have some around the house. I find that *Sobo* is best, but any good glue that adheres to fabric will fill the bill.

Bits of yarn, a few sequins, and wooden hangers can all be used for at least some of the designs. You may find some other commonplace items around the house that may prove useful—cardboard, empty frozen-juice cans, tracing paper, a tape measure, and others.

Whatever you are lacking can be obtained at a neighborhood notions shop or local five-and-dime store.

After much struggling to cut out the tiny eyes which are paired on all the beanbags, hand puppets, and many of the other items, I finally discovered that an inexpensive hole puncher (the kind that students use to make paper fit into their loose-leaf binders) does the trick in nothing flat. Since those dots are the smallest and most frequently used felt decoration, I think it is a wise investment. Besides, the hole puncher can always be useful for other things—like cutting holes in paper.

Another item you'll need is inexpensive construction paper and some tracing or lightweight typing paper for making the outlines of the designs. I prefer typing paper for this purpose, because tracing paper is just too delicate for outlining the designs and tends to tear. If you place a piece of typing paper over any of the designs in this book, you'll see how clearly the outline shows through.

If you are just going to make one or two items of the same pattern, you won't need the construction paper. You merely outline the design on the typing paper, cut out all the paper parts, and pin them onto the felt. Then you cut the designs out of the felt. However, if you are planning to make a dozen items in one design, it is best to transfer your design from the typing paper to a piece of stiffer construction paper. Then, you can cut out the pattern in the heavier construction paper and lay it right on the felt. This takes a few minutes longer, but in the long run it will prove to be a time-saver because you don't have to pin the pattern to the felt—you can *draw* the outline directly onto the material in pencil.

The hole puncher and the pattern paper you decide upon are available in a five-and-dime store or at any stationery store.

To stuff the beanbags, you'll need beans, of course, and for those, you'll go over to the grocer's. There is one very important reason why I recommend navy beans for the beanbags: *they are edible.* If a small tot wanders into your work area and pops a bean into his mouth—he's actually had a little bit of his dinner and no harm done. And if a young recipient of one of the beanbags manages to rip it open (which is difficult) and decides to munch a few beans, he'll not be harmed.

Besides the safety factor, navy beans are available and inexpensive. And if you have some left over, there is always bean soup.

Now, you've picked your designs, checked your supplies, and gone off to the store to buy what you need. Don't forget the felt.

As I mentioned, felt is supplied to notions stores in

9 × 12-inch rectangles. Each of the designs shown in this book can be made from no more than *two* of these rectangles. Many of the smaller designs can be made from just one piece of felt.

For example, with two 9 × 12-inch pieces of felt, you can make three mouse beanbags or four comb cases or twelve key chains or eighteen bookmarks. Considering that the cost of one felt rectangle is about 20 cents, you can see how inexpensive these designs are to make, either for yourself or as gifts. (Prices vary slightly in different parts of the country.)

When you buy the felt, remember to buy *two* pieces of the exact same color if you are planning to make beanbags, hand puppets, dolls' dresses, glove or handkerchief cases, etc. The remaining items in this book can be made with just one piece of felt. And you can manufacture virtually hundreds of eyes, ears, noses, and other necessary parts from just a single piece of felt.

Since felt has no "wrong" side, it can be steam-ironed to remove wrinkles. And if you get a stain on one side, you can just turn it over to the other side and use that for your "showing" surface.

Always save your scraps of felt. The smallest smidgen can be useful. You can use the tiniest scraps for eyes, noses, mouths, ears, decorations, borders, and the like. And almost any scrap from 4 to 7 inches long and 1 inch wide will make a very respectable bookmark.

Again, if you are planning to make any design in large quantities, it would be cheaper to buy your felt by the yard. If this is your plan because you are going to make, say, 50 chicken beanbags, then you will need several yards of yellow felt, but only a small amount of orange for the beaks and feet. (If your notions shop doesn't sell felt by the yard, try a fabric store or the yard-goods section of a department store.)

Find a large surface—a dining-room table, maybe—to work on; cut your pattern out in construction or typing paper, and lay it down on the felt. If you do several at a time, you'll find you will use your felt more efficiently because you will be able to take advantage of odd-shaped little areas that otherwise might go to waste. By placing the pattern in different positions on the material, you can figure out ways to squeeze as much as possible out of the yardage.

Naturally, it's preferable to sew the designs by machine.

It's faster and the end product will be stronger. However, *all* the patterns in this book can be sewn by hand. The hangers, for example, were sewn by hand (both the decorations and the hangers themselves) and a very nice effect was achieved with a simple running stitch. So, if you don't have a sewing machine, don't worry. It isn't essential.

When sewing any pattern where you must stop, stuff, and then sew up to close, reinforce the areas where the thread has been broken for the opening with extra stitching. This is especially important for the beanbags. It also helps to reinforce the corners of the hand puppets, which will get a lot of stress when hands are constantly going in and out of the opening.

When you paste the different parts of the patterns onto the main part, be very stingy with the glue. Most fabric glues dry clear (be sure the one you're using does), and the tiniest speck is all that's needed to glue an eye or a button in place. It might be wise to experiment first with glue on a scrap of felt. Just make sure to cover the entire surface of the small part you are pasting onto the main or larger part. Press down a moment and then allow it to dry.

Before pasting in place the smallest parts (eyes, ears, noses, clipboard decorations, etc.) position them first so that you can see how the finished product will look. This is especially important for faces, which should be as symmetrical as possible. If some parts are to be sewn onto the main part, always pin them in place first.

Since *all* of the patterns described in this book require glue and a pair of scissors, these two items will not be listed under the heading "materials needed" for each design. Just remember—you need them!

If you decide to pencil the outline of the pattern onto the felt rather than pin it on, you may find a trace of pencil mark on the felt after you have cut out the pattern. Just turn both pieces over so the parts match back to back and proceed to finish the item.

In the directions for each pattern, when a piece of 9 × 12-inch felt will make *more than one completed design*, it is so indicated under the heading "materials needed."

When only one rectangle is required—and the pattern must be cut in two thicknesses, as in the pincushions—it is usually best to cut the rectangle in half before cutting or tracing the pattern. It seems to work better than just *folding* the felt rectangle in half.

Any beanbag can be stuffed with cotton instead of beans and used as a crib toy, small cushion, or wall decoration. And without any stuffing, the beanbag patterns (only one thickness, of course) can be used to decorate bedspreads, curtains, aprons, tunics, shorts, skirts, belts, vests or whatever.

All of the decorative designs suggested for the clipboards and bookmarks can be used interchangeably for almost any of the other patterns. Paste a garden of tulips on a doll's dress or dried-flower holder. Use the same design on a comb case, eyeglass case, handkerchief case, and scissors case for a handsome, matching travel gift. Change the hanger decorations into mobiles by omitting the cotton stuffing and pasting the parts together instead of sewing them together. Cover the pencil holder with mushrooms and turn it into a spoon holder for the kitchen. In other words, don't be restricted by the suggestions here.

And remember that all the eyes, noses, buttons, and most mouths are interchangeable.

I think you're ready to start now. Pick a pattern — get comfortable — and go ahead.

2. beanbags

general instructions for making all beanbags

1. All beanbag bodies are made from two 9 × 12-inch rectangles of the same color felt. For each design, "pieces of felt" refers to 9 × 12-inch rectangles. When the word "scrap" appears, it means that only a small piece of that particular color is needed. (You can judge the amount needed by the pattern requirement of that color for eyes, ears, noses, etc.) There is no pattern for ¼-inch eyes; simply punch them out with a hole puncher.

2. Trace the body outline of the pattern on one piece of felt. Then, making sure the two pieces of felt for the body are exactly aligned, cut out the two pieces at the same time. This makes sure that both sides match perfectly and you need only draw the pattern once.

3. Always use a large pair of scissors to cut out the body of the beanbag, a smaller pair of scissors for the other parts.

4. Paste the small parts (eyes, nose, mouth, etc.) onto the body *before* sewing. Put the glue on the *small* part, not the body.

5. Pin or paste parts like ears and tails in place before sewing. Pin the two parts of the beanbag together before sewing them.

6. Do not overstuff the beanbag with beans. If you do, you will have trouble sewing up the opening.

7. Reinforce the sides of the opening after the beanbag is stuffed and sewn together. Then, cut off all loose ends of thread. Remove all pins.

CHICKEN BEANBAG

materials needed

2 pieces of yellow felt for the body (makes 2 beanbags)
1 scrap of orange felt for the beak and feet
1 scrap of black felt for ¼-inch eyes
   yellow thread to match
¾ cup of navy beans for each beanbag

directions

1. Trace the outline of the chicken body (A) on the yellow felt and outline of beak (C) and 2 feet (B) on the orange felt.

2. Cut out the 2 yellow body outlines with pinking shears, if available. Cut out 1 beak and 2 feet from orange felt using a straight pair of scissors. Cut or punch out 2 black eyes.

3. Pin the 2 sides of the body together.

4. Paste the beak between the 2 parts of the body as indicated in the composite diagram on this page. Do the same with the feet. Paste the eyes on the sides of the head as indicated.

5. Sew the beanbag all around, starting below the beak, going around the head, and continuing to just beyond the feet. Leave a 3-inch opening.

6. Pour the beans into the opening.

7. Finish by sewing up the opening and removing pins.

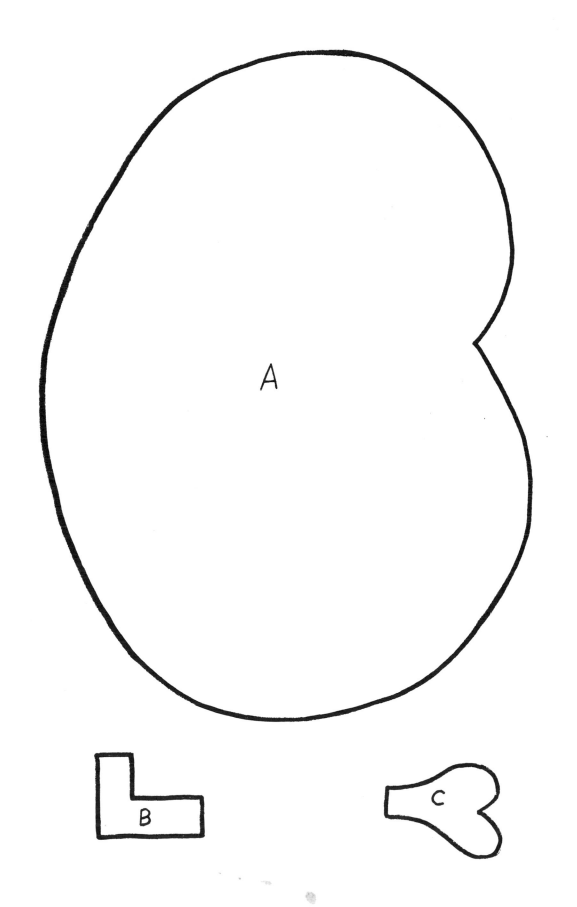

MOUSE BEANBAG

materials needed

2 pieces of purple felt for the body (makes 3 beanbags)
1 piece of red felt for the ears and tail
1 scrap of black felt for ¼-inch eyes
    purple thread to match
²/₃ cup of navy beans
        for each beanbag

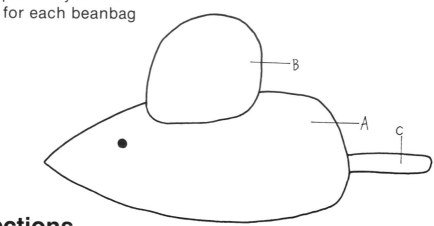

directions

1. Trace the outline of the mouse body (A) on the purple felt and the outline of the 2 ears (B) and tail (C) on the red felt.

2. Cut out the 2 purple body outlines with pinking shears, if you have them. Cut out 2 red ears and 1 red tail with straight scissors. Punch or cut out 2 black eyes.

3. Pin the 2 sides of the body together.

4. Paste an eye on each side of the mouse's head, as shown in the composite diagram on this page. Paste the ears on the outside of the body, as shown (about 2½ inches from the tip of the nose). Paste the tail between the 2 rounded ends of the body, inserting it about ½ inch inside.

5. Sew the beanbag all around, starting at the nose, over the ears and tail, and stopping at the underside. Leave a 3-inch opening.

6. Pour the beans into the opening.

7. Finish by sewing up the opening and removing pins.

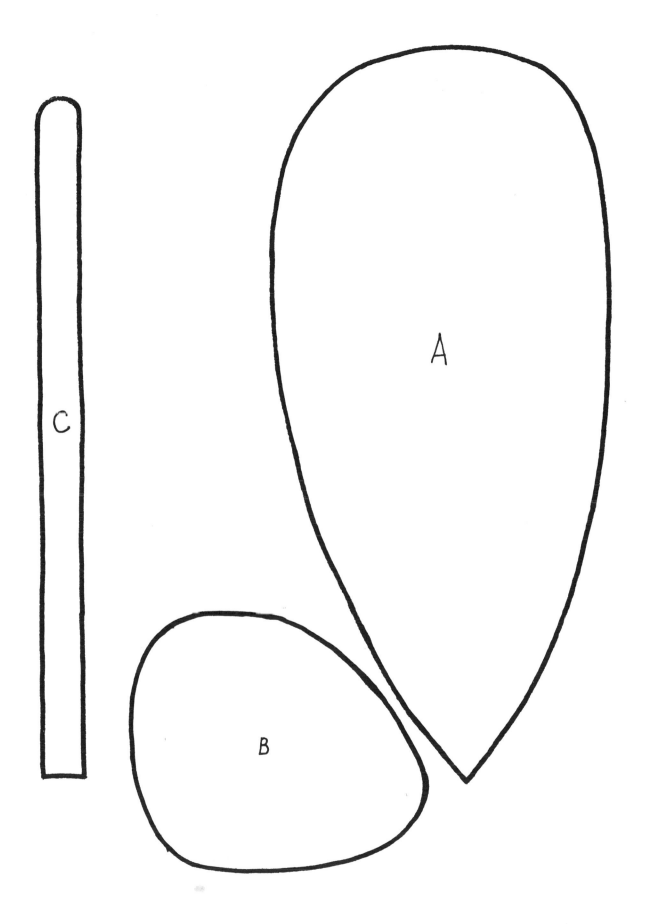

ARTIST'S PALETTE BEANBAG

materials needed

1 piece of brown felt for the body (makes 2 beanbags)
1 scrap each of red, pink, blue, orange, yellow, and green felt
    brown thread to match
½ cup of navy beans

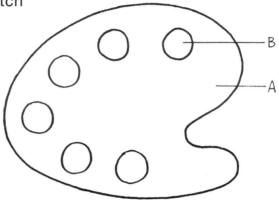

directions

1. Trace 2 outlines of the palette (A) on the brown felt. Trace the outline of the circle (B) on each scrap of colored felt, a total of 6.

2. Cut out 2 brown palette sides. Cut out the 6 colored circles.

3. Pin the 2 sides of the palette together.

4. Paste one circle of any color in one corner of the palette; lay the others out, spaced evenly as shown in the composite diagram on this page. Now paste them in place.

5. Sew the palette all around, starting at the top of the curve. Leave a 3-inch opening.

6. Pour the beans into the opening.

7. Finish by sewing up the opening and removing pins.

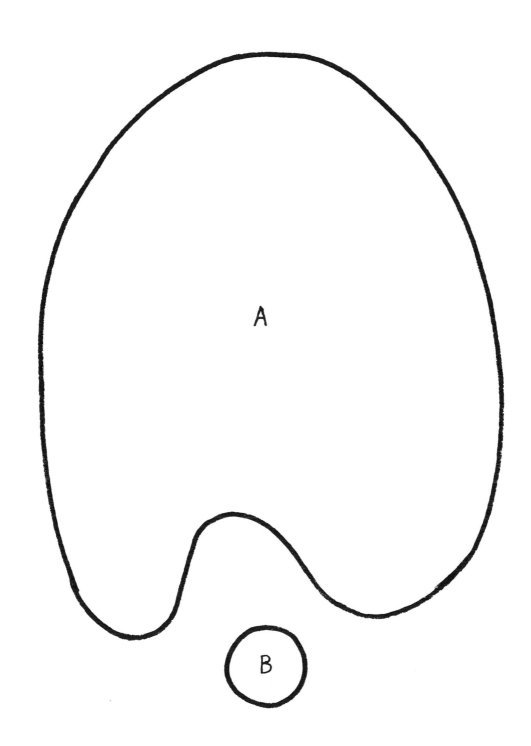

OWL BEANBAG

materials needed

2 pieces of dark gray felt for the body (makes 2 beanbags)
1 scrap each of yellow, white, and black felt
    gray thread to match
¾ cup of navy beans

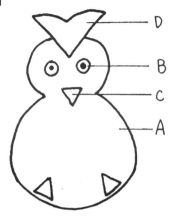

directions

1. Trace the outline of the owl (A) on the gray felt. Trace the outline of 1 large triangle (D) and 3 small triangles (C) on the yellow felt. Trace the outline of 2 circles (B) on the white felt.

2. Cut out 2 gray owl bodies and 3 small yellow triangles. Cut out the large yellow triangle with pinking shears, if you have them. Cut out 2 white circles. Cut or punch out 2 black dots.

3. Pin the 2 sides of the body together.

4. Paste the large yellow triangle in the center of the head so that the winglike parts stick up, as shown in composite diagram on this page. Paste the 2 white circles in place, as shown. Paste 1 yellow triangle in place for the nose and the other 2 in place for the feet, as shown. Now paste a black dot on each white circle for the eyes.

5. Sew the beanbag all around, starting at one side of the head and continuing all around the head and body. Leave a 3-inch opening.

6. Pour the beans into the opening.

7. Finish by sewing up the opening and removing pins.

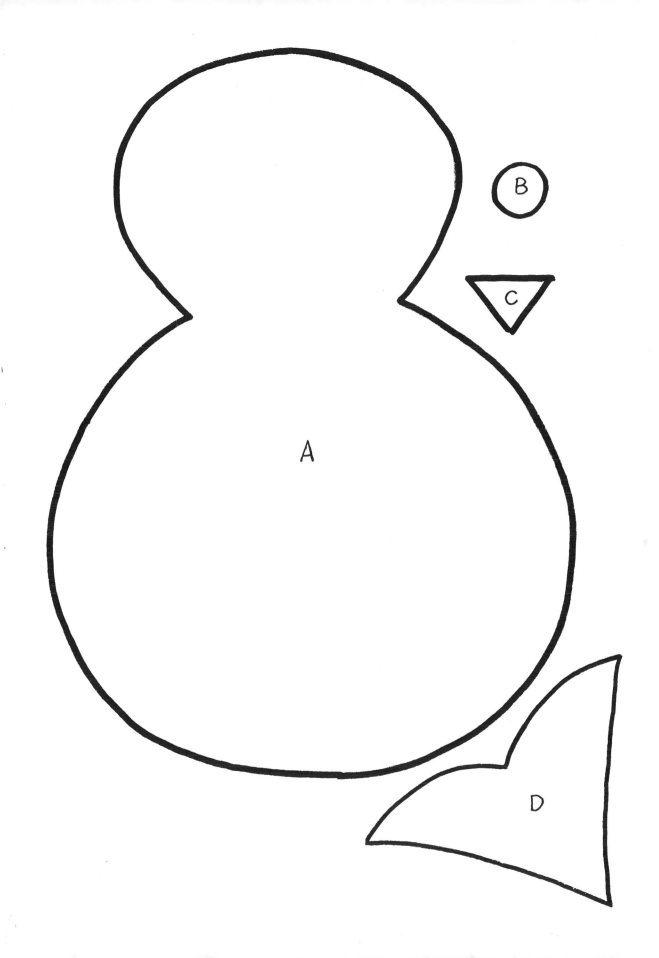

A

B

C

D

GINGERBREAD BOY BEANBAG

materials needed

2 pieces of brown felt for the body
1 scrap each of orange, red, white, and black felt for ½-inch
    circles
  white thread to match
1 cup of navy beans

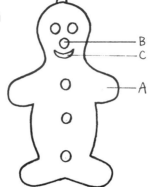

directions

1. Trace the outline of the gingerbread boy body (A) on the brown felt. Trace the mouth (C) on red felt. Trace three orange circles (B), 2 black, 1 red, and 1 white on the scraps of felt (you can use a dime instead of the pattern for the circles).

2. Cut out 2 brown body outlines. Cut out the red mouth and colored circles.

3. Pin the 2 sides of the body together.

4. Paste the dots on the body as shown in the composite diagram on this page. Use black for the eyes, white for the nose, orange for the buttons. Paste the red dot at the top of the head, halfway in between the 2 body parts. Paste the mouth in position.

5. Sew the beanbag all around, starting under one arm, around the head and other arm, and stopping just beyond the feet. Leave a 3-inch opening.

6. Pour the beans into the opening.

7. Finish by sewing up the opening and removing the pins.

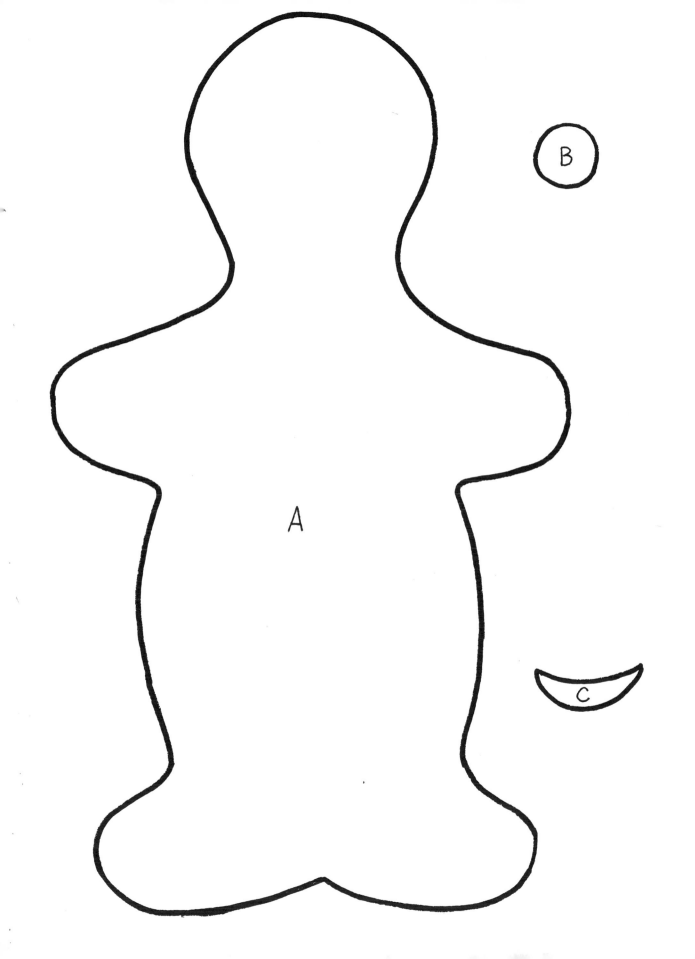

A

B

C

DUCK BEANBAG

materials needed

2 pieces of dark yellow felt for the body (makes 2 beanbags)
1 scrap each of orange and black felt
   yellow thread to match
1/3 cup of beans

directions

1. Trace the outline of the duck (A) on the yellow felt. Trace the outline of the beak (B) and feet (C) on the orange felt.

2. Cut out 2 yellow duck bodies. Cut out 2 feet and 1 beak. Cut or punch out 2 black eyes.

3. Pin the 2 sides of the body together. Pink the ends of the tail.

4. Paste the beak in between the 2 parts of the head, as shown in the composite diagram on this page. Do the same with the 2 feet. Paste an eye on each side of the head, as indicated.

5. Sew the beanbag all around, starting behind the head, continuing around the head and beak, and stopping just beyond the tail. Leave a 3-inch opening.

6. Pour the beans into the opening.

7. Finish by sewing up the opening and removing pins.

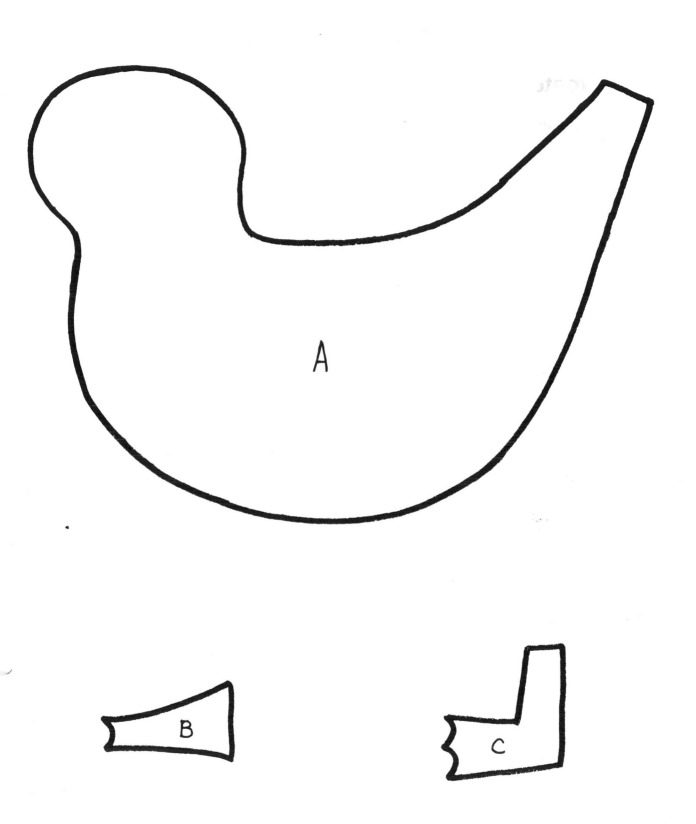

A

B

C

CLOWN BEANBAG

materials needed

2 pieces of shocking pink felt for the body
1 scrap each of black, white, red, yellow, and blue felt
    pink thread to match
¾ cup of navy beans

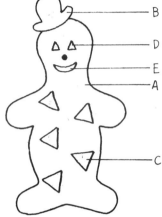

directions

1. Trace the outline of the clown body (A) on the pink felt. Trace the outline of the large triangle (C) once each on the black, white, red, yellow, and blue felt scraps. Trace 2 small triangles (D) on the black felt. Trace the mouth (E) on the red felt. Trace the hat (B) on the blue felt.

2. Cut out the 2 pink body outlines. Cut out 1 large triangle in each color. Cut out 2 small black triangles for the eyes. Cut out 1 red mouth and 1 blue hat. Cut or punch out 1 white dot for the nose.

3. Pin the 2 sides of the body together.

4. For eyes, paste the 2 small black triangles on the face, as shown in the composite diagram on this page. Paste the nose and mouth in place, as shown. Paste the hat on the front part of the head, as shown. Paste the large triangles around the body in an uneven pattern.

5. Sew the beanbag all around, starting under one arm, going around the head and other arm, stopping just beyond the feet. Leave a 2½-inch opening.

6. Pour the beans into the opening.

7. Finish by sewing up the opening and removing all pins.

SNOWMAN BEANBAG

materials needed

2 pieces of white felt for the body (makes 2 beanbags)
1 scrap of black felt
1 scrap of red felt
   white thread to match
¾ cup of navy beans

directions

1. Trace the outline of the snowman body (A) on the white felt and the outlines of the hat (B) and pipe (C) on the black felt. Trace the mouth (E) and buttons (D) on the red felt.

2. Cut out 2 white body outlines. Cut out 2 hats, 2 eyes, and 1 pipe in black. Cut out the mouth and 3 buttons in red felt. Cut or punch out 2 black eyes.

3. Pin the 2 sides of the body together.

4. Paste the eyes and buttons on the body, as shown in the composite diagram on this page. Paste the pipe on the face as indicated, allowing it to dry, and then pasting the mouth *over* the stem of the pipe.

5. Sew the beanbag all around, starting at one side of the head and continuing around the head and body. Leave a 3-inch opening.

6. Pour the beans into the opening.

7. Sew up the opening, removing pins.

8. Paste the top of the hat together, making sure both sides match perfectly. Leave the brim open for the moment. Now paste the brim on the front and back of the head, as shown.

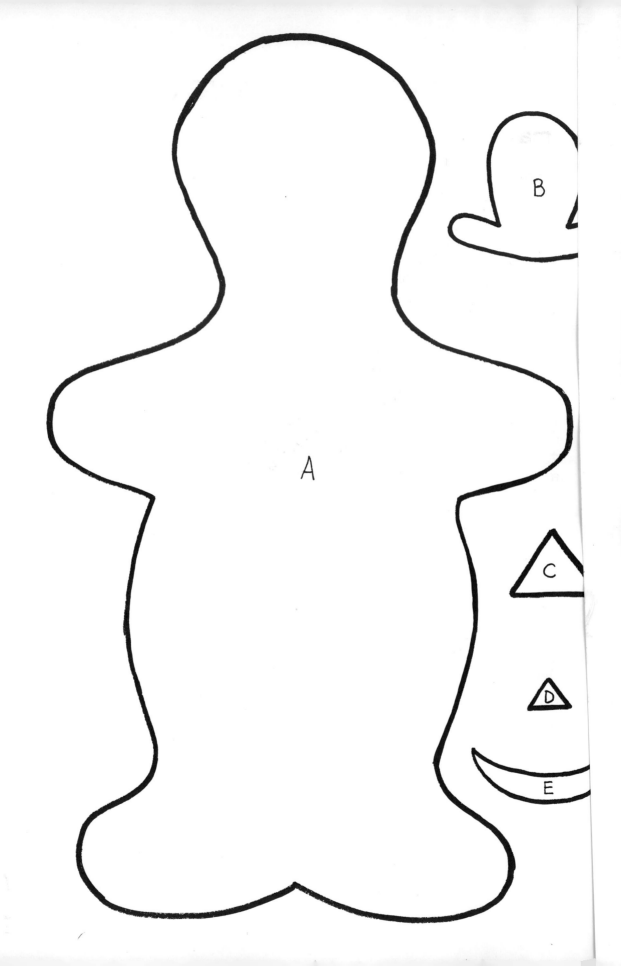

MUSHROOM BEANBAG

materials needed

1 piece of red felt (makes 3 beanbags)
1 piece of white felt
   red thread to match
¾ cup of navy beans

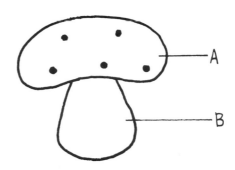

directions

1. Trace the outline of the mushroom top on the red felt. Trace the outline of the bottom of the mushroom on the white felt.

2. Cut out 2 red tops and 2 white bottoms. Cut or punch out 10 white ¼-inch dots.

3. Pin 1 red top over 1 white bottom so that the red part overlaps the white part about ½ inch (see the composite diagram on this page). Repeat with the other red top and white bottom.

4. Sew the red pieces to the white pieces to make the 2 sides of the mushroom.

5. Pin the 2 sides together. Make sure they are exactly even.

6. Paste 5 white dots on each side of the mushroom top, as shown.

7. Sew the beanbag all around, starting under the top, going around the top, and down one side. Leave a 3-inch opening.

8. Pour the beans into the opening.

9. Finish by sewing up the opening and removing pins.

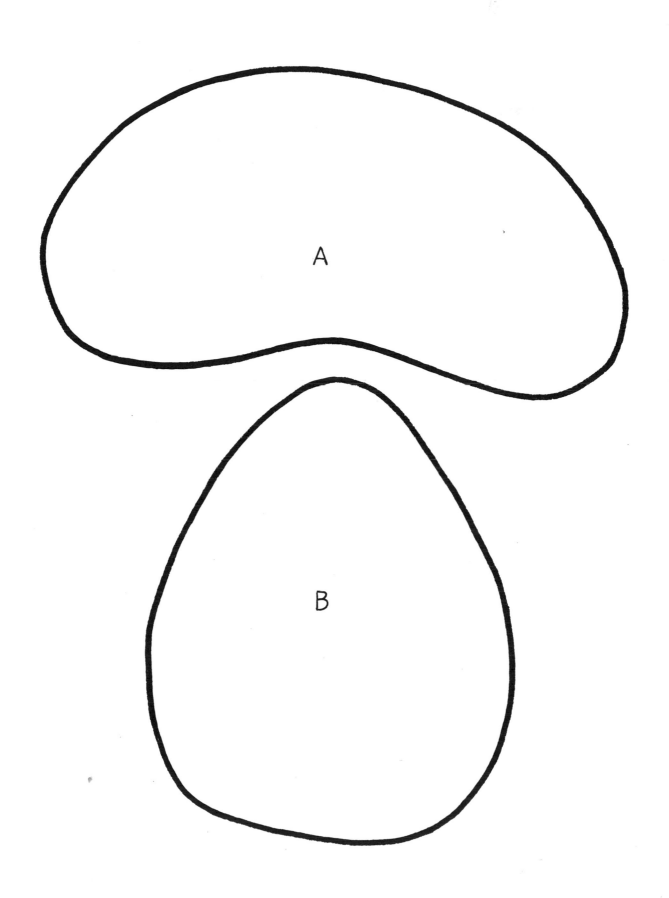

SANTA CLAUS BEANBAG

materials needed

2 pieces of red felt for the body (makes 2 beanbags)
1 scrap each of white and black felt
   red thread
¾ cup of navy beans

directions

1. Trace the outline of the Santa Claus (A) on the red felt. Trace the outline of the hat (F) on the red felt. Trace the outline of the beard (C), hands (E), hatband (G), and circle (B) on the white felt. Trace the outline of the mouth (D) on the black felt.

2. Cut out 2 red Santa Claus bodies, 2 red hats, 2 white hands, 1 white beard, 1 white hatband, 1 white circle, and 1 black mouth. Cut or punch out 2 ¼-inch black dots for eyes and 1 ¼-inch white dot.

3. Pin the 2 sides of the body together.

4. Paste the 2 black eyes in place, as shown in the composite diagram on this page. Paste the white beard, the 2 white hands, and the white circle as a nose in place, as shown. Paste the black mouth over the beard, as shown. Paste 2 parts of the hat together, at the top, making sure both sides match evenly. Leave the brim open for the moment. Now paste the brim onto the front and back of the head, as shown. Paste a ¼-inch white dot on the tip of the hat.

5. Sew the beanbag all around, starting at one side of the head and continuing around the hat, the head, and the body. Leave a 3-inch opening.

6. Pour the beans into the opening.

7. Sew up the opening, removing the pins.

8. Paste the hatband across the bottom of the hat, as shown.

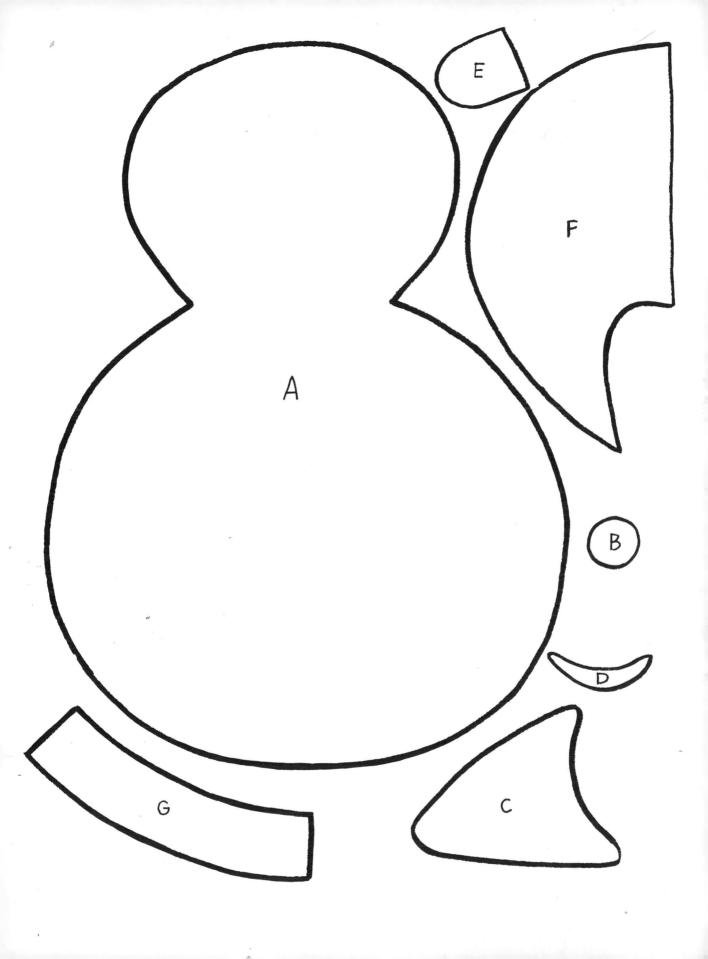

BUTTERFLY BEANBAG

materials needed

2 pieces of red felt for the wings
1 scrap of blue felt for the body
1 scrap of white felt for ¼-inch dots
   red thread to match
1 cup of navy beans

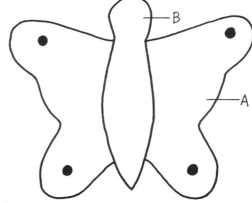

directions

1. Trace the outline of the butterfly wings (A) on the red felt. Trace the outline of the butterfly body (B) on the blue felt.

2. Cut out 2 red wings and 2 blue bodies. Cut or punch out 8 ¼-inch white dots.

3. Pin the 2 sides of the wings together.

4. Glue 1 blue body down the center of the wings so that the head and tail stick out above and below, as shown in the composite diagram on this page. Now cover the second blue body entirely with a thin layer of glue and position it on the underside of the wings, pressing the 2 heads and 2 tails together first so that they meet perfectly. Paste a white dot on the tip of each of the wings—on both sides.

5. Sew the beanbag all around, starting at the head, continuing through the head, around the wings, through the tail around the other wings, and stopping so as to leave a 3-inch opening.

6. Pour the beans into the opening.

7. Finish by sewing up the opening and removing the pins.

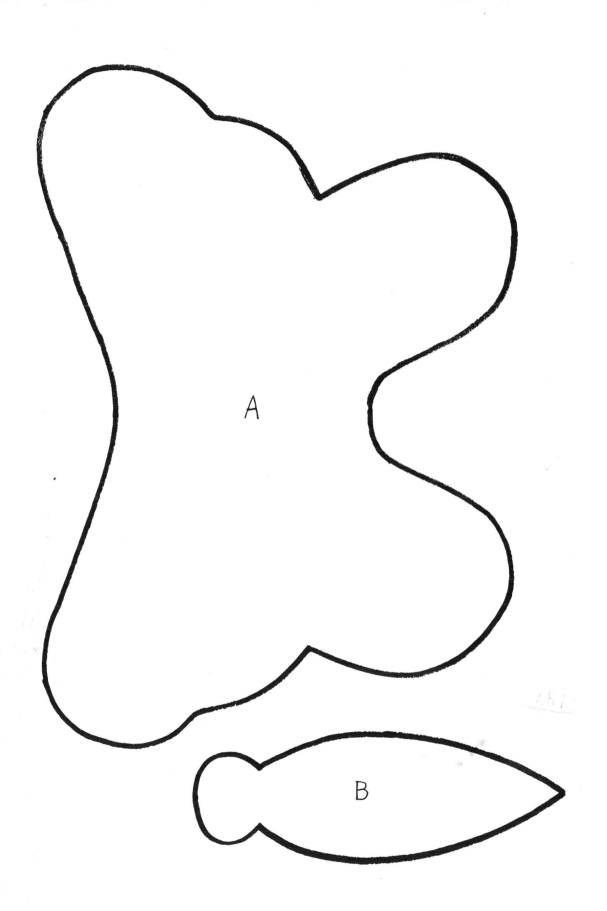

A

B

TEDDY BEAR BEANBAG
(mama bear*)

materials needed

2 pieces of brown felt for the body
1 scrap each of yellow, white, and black felt for
    the eyes, nose-mouth, and paws
  brown thread
1 cup of navy beans

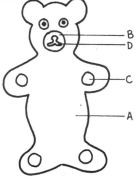

directions

1. Trace the outline of the teddy bear body (A) on the brown felt. Trace the ½-inch circle (C) on the yellow and white felt. Trace the 1-inch circle (B) on the yellow felt. Trace the nose-mouth (D) on the black felt.

2. Cut out 2 brown bear bodies with pinking shears, if available. Cut out 4 yellow ½-inch circles and 1 yellow 1-inch circle. Cut out 2 white ½-inch circles. Cut out the nose-mouth in black. Cut or punch out 2 ¼-inch black dots.

3. Pin the 2 sides of the body together.

4. Paste the 2 whites of the eyes (½-inch circles) in place, as shown in the composite diagram on this page. Allow to dry. Paste the 1-inch yellow circle just below the eyes, as shown. Allow to dry. Paste the 4 yellow ½-inch circles on each paw, as shown. Now, paste a black dot in the center of each eye circle. Paste the nose-mouth over the circle on the face.

5. Sew the beanbag all around, starting under one arm, going around the arm, over the head, down the side, and around the feet. Leave a 3-inch opening.

6. Pour the beans into the opening.

7. Finish by sewing up the opening and removing pins.

* For a complete bear family, see patterns on pages 48 and 66.

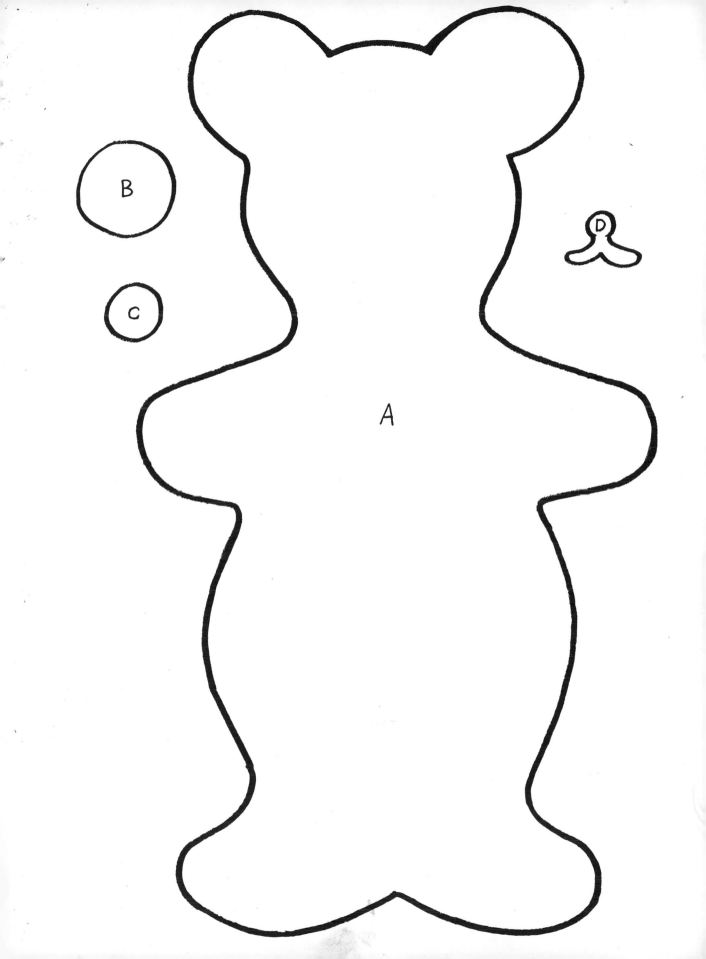

FAWN BEANBAG

materials needed

2 pieces of gold-colored felt for the body
1 scrap each of brown, red, black, and white felt
  gold thread to match
1 cup of navy beans

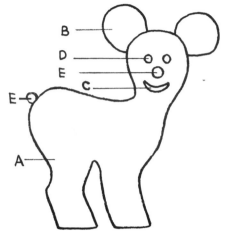

directions

1. Trace the outline of the fawn (A) on the gold felt. Trace the ears (B) on the brown felt. Trace the ½-inch circle (D) on the black felt and the ⅝-inch circle (E) on the red and white felt. Trace the mouth (C) on the red felt.

2. Cut out 2 gold fawn bodies. Cut out 2 brown ears. Cut out 1 red circle and 1 white circle. Cut out the mouth in red. Cut or punch out 2 ¼-inch circles for eyes.

3. Pin the 2 sides of the body together.

4. Insert the straight part of the ear about ½-inch between the 2 body layers and paste (see the composite diagram on this page for position). Ears should tilt slightly and be about 1¾-inches apart. Paste the black eyes, red nose, and mouth in place, as shown. For the tail, paste the white circle halfway in, between the 2 body layers as shown.

5. Sew the beanbag all around, starting at the right side of the head, continuing around the head (leave ears free except to secure at head) until just beyond the tail. Leave a 3-inch opening.

6. Pour beans into opening.

7. Finish by sewing up opening and removing pins.

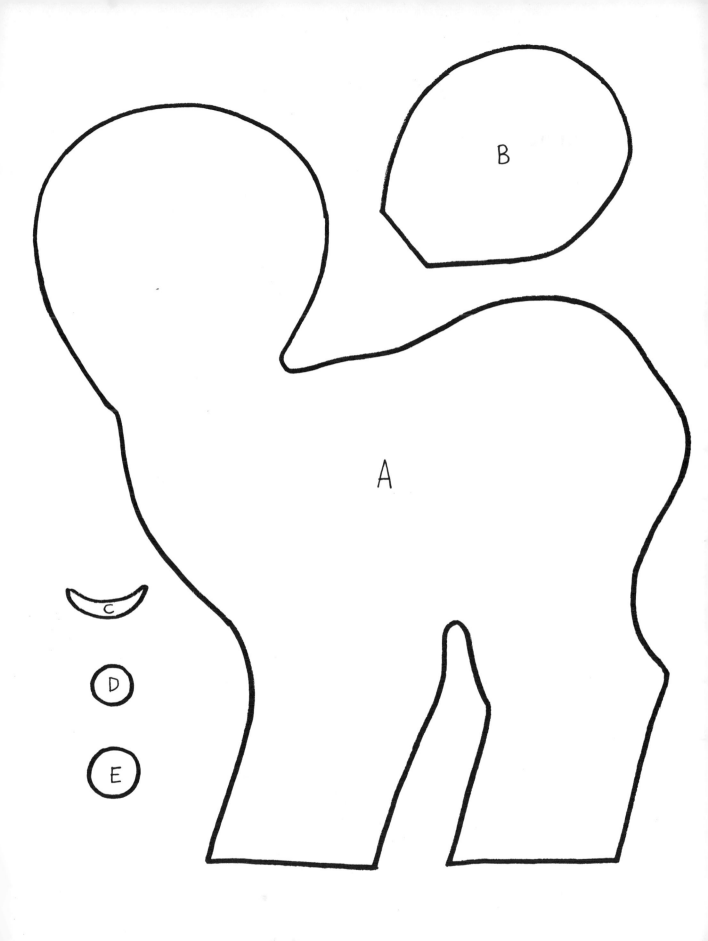

SEAL BEANBAG

materials needed

2 pieces of purple felt for the body
1 scrap of orange felt for the ball
1 scrap of black felt
   purple thread to match
½ cup of navy beans

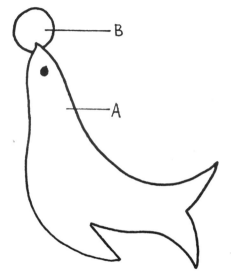

directions

1. Trace the outline of the seal body (A) on the purple felt. Trace the ball (B) on the orange felt (note that the ball has a tab).

2. Cut out 2 purple body outlines with pinking shears, if available. Cut out 2 orange balls with a straight scissors. Cut or punch out 2 black eyes.

3. Pin the 2 sides of the body together.

4. Paste the 2 orange balls together and let dry. Then, paste the squared tab of the ball into the mouth of the seal, between the 2 body pieces, so that only the round part will be exposed. For position see the composite diagram on this page. Paste an eye on each side of the head.

5. Sew the beanbag all around, starting at the neck, going around the nose, and continuing to just beyond the fins. Leave a 3-inch opening.

6. Pour the beans into the opening. Be sure to get the beans into the fin and tail (pour and stuff fin; pour and stuff tail).

7. Finish by sewing up the opening and removing pins.

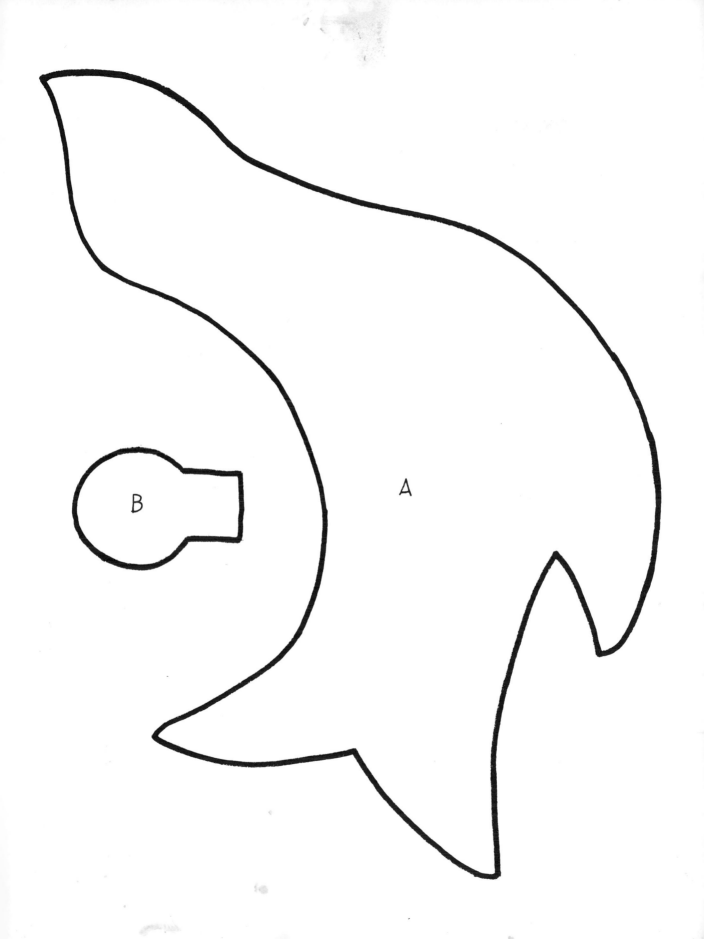

FANCY FROG BEANBAG

materials needed

1 piece of yellow felt for the body (makes 2 beanbags)
1 piece of green felt for the body
1 scrap each of white and black felt
10 ¼-inch sequins, assorted colors
    green thread to match
¾ cup of navy beans

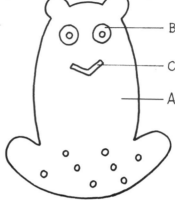

directions

1. Trace the outline of the frog (A) on the yellow felt. Trace the outline of the circle (B) on the white felt. Trace the mouth (C) on the black felt.

2. Place the piece of yellow felt exactly on top of the piece of green felt and cut out 2 frog outlines. Cut out 2 white circles. Cut out 1 black mouth.

3. Pin the 2 sides of the beanbag together.

4. Paste the 2 white circles in place on the yellow frog body part, as shown in the composite diagram on this page. Paste the mouth in place, as shown. Paste a green sequin in the center of each white circle. Paste 8 more sequins around the bottom of the frog, as shown.

5. Sew the beanbag all around, starting at the top of one leg, going around the bottom, up one side, and around the ears. Leave a 3-inch opening.

6. Pour the beans into the beanbag.

7. Finish by sewing up the opening and removing the pins.

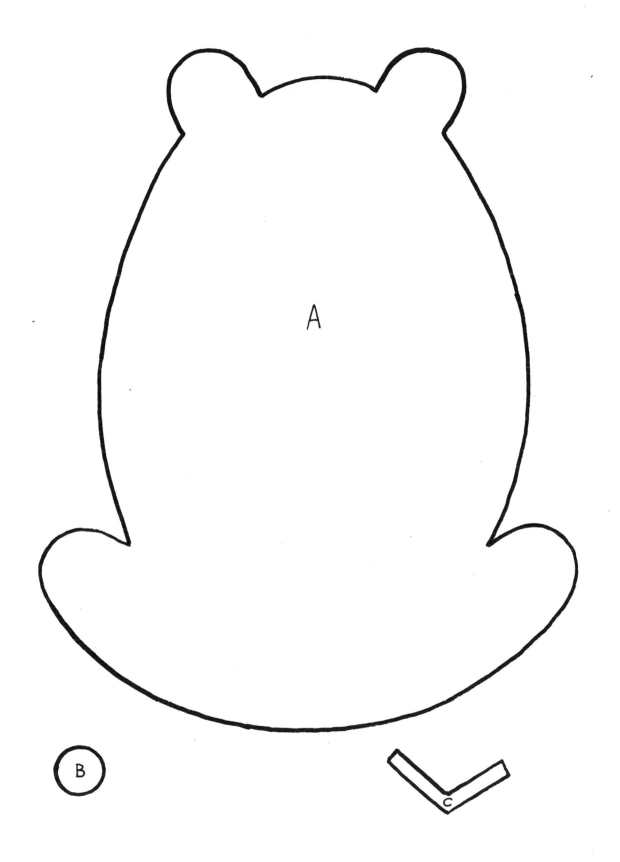

LADYBUG BEANBAG

materials needed

2 pieces of red felt for the body (makes 2 beanbags)
1 scrap of black felt
   black thread
¾ cup of navy beans

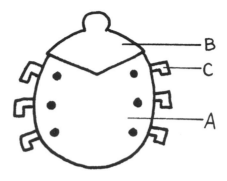

directions

1. Trace the body of the ladybug (A) on the red felt. Trace the 1-piece head and shoulder outline (B) on the black felt. Trace the foot (C) on the black felt.

2. Cut out 2 red bodies. Cut out 1 head and shoulder part. Cut out 6 black feet. Cut or punch out 6 ¼-inch black dots.

3. Pin the 2 sides of the body together.

4. Lay out all parts on the body before pasting, to make sure the positions are as shown in the composite diagram on this page. Now paste the 6 black dots in place. Next, insert each leg about ¼ inch in between the two parts of the body, lining them up with each black dot. Paste them in place. Finally, paste the head-shoulder part onto the body, as shown, making sure the head protrudes over the edge of the body freely.

5. Sew the beanbag all around, starting under one leg, continuing around all the legs on that side, around the shoulder, and around the other 3 legs. Leave a 3-inch opening.

6. Pour the beans into the opening.

7. Finish by sewing up the opening and removing pins.

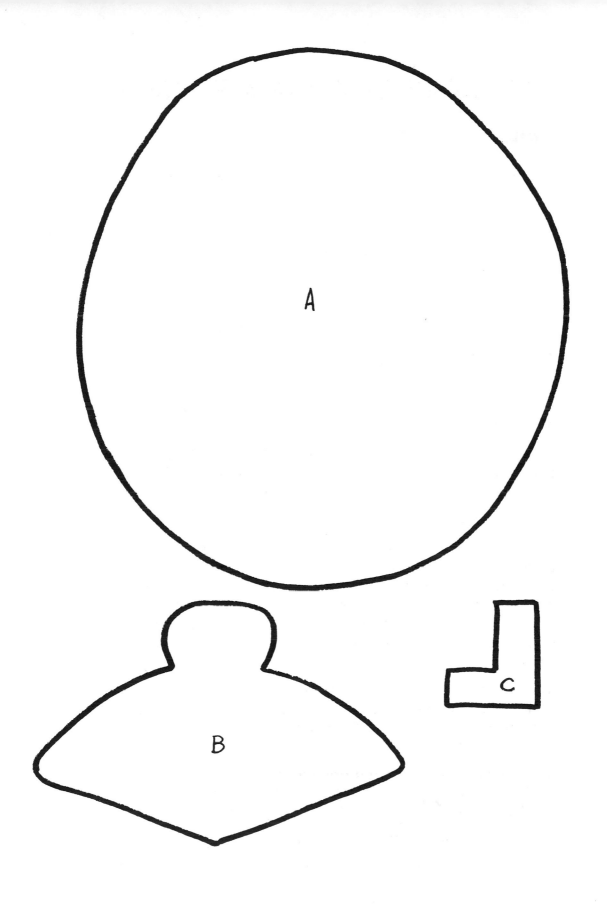

A

B

C

CIRCUS ELEPHANT BEANBAG

materials needed

2 pieces of shocking pink felt for the body (makes 2
    beanbags)
1 scrap each of light blue and royal blue felt
11 sequins (¼-inch) in assorted colors
    shocking pink thread to match
½ cup of navy beans

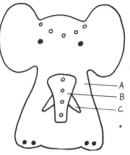

directions

1. Trace the outline of the elephant (A) on the pink felt.
Trace the outline of the trunk (B) and the tusk (C) on the light
blue felt.

2. Cut out 2 pink elephant bodies. Cut out 1 light blue trunk
and 2 light blue tusks. Cut or punch out 4 light blue ¼-inch
dots. Cut or punch out 2 royal blue ¼-inch dots for eyes.

3. Pin the 2 sides of the body together.

4. Paste the 2 light blue tusks in place, as shown in the
composite diagram on this page. Note that their position is
underneath the trunk part. While they are drying, paste the
4 light blue dots in place, as shown, 2 on each hoof. Paste the
2 royal blue eyes in place. Now paste the light blue trunk
in place over the tusks, leaving all but ½ inch of each tusk
showing.

5. Paste the sequins on the elephant in the following pattern:
1 sequin on the tip of each tusk; 4 sequins down the front of
the trunk, evenly spaced; 5 sequins pasted near the top of the
head in a semicircle.

6. Sew the beanbag all around, starting under one ear,
continuing around the top of the head, down the side, and
across the bottom. Leave a 3-inch opening.

7. Pour the beans into the opening.

8. Finish by sewing up the opening and removing the pins.

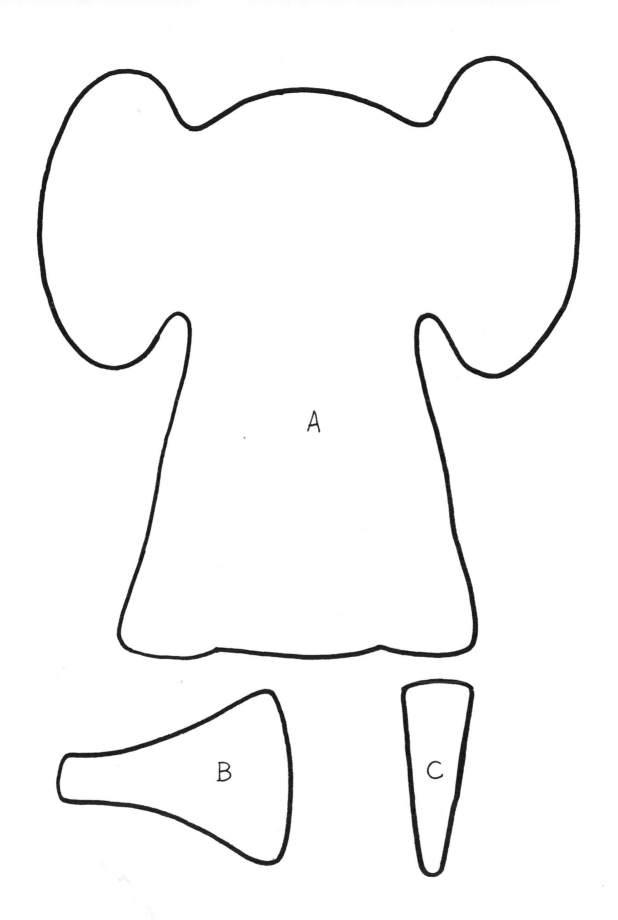

SHIMMERING SEAHORSE BEANBAG

materials needed

2 pieces of dark green felt for the body (makes 2 beanbags)
1 scrap each of black, white, and orange felt
    about 3 dozen sequins
    orange thread to match
½ cup of navy beans

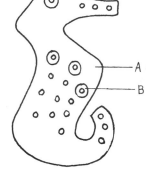

directions

1. Trace the outline of the seahorse body (A) on the green felt. Trace the outline of the circle (B) on both the orange and white felt.

2. Cut out 2 green body outlines with pinking shears, if available. Cut out 6 orange circles and 2 white circles. Cut or punch out 2 black ¼-inch dots. Use straight scissors for all circles.

3. Pin the 2 sides of the body together.

4. Paste 3 orange circles on each side of the body, as shown in the composite diagram on this page. Paste 1 white circle for "white" of eye on each side, as shown. Paste a black "eye" dot on top of each white circle.

5. Sew the beanbag all around, starting under the neck, going around the head, down the back, around the tail, and up to the belly. Leave a 3-inch opening.

6. Paste the sequins all over both sides of the body for scales.

7. Pour the beans into the opening. Be sure you get the beans into the head and tail. (Pour and stuff the tail; pour and stuff the head.)

8. Finish by sewing up the opening and removing pins.

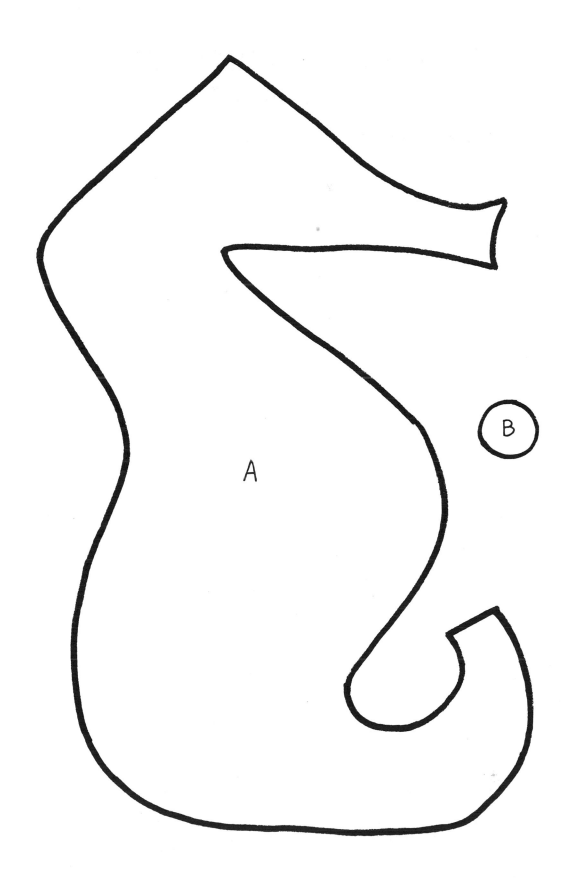

TEDDY BEAR STUFFED TOY
(baby bear*)

materials needed

2 pieces of brown felt for the body (makes 4 teddy bears)
1 scrap each of orange and black felt
   brown thread to match
   cotton for stuffing

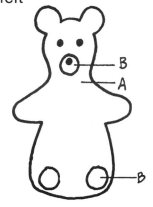

directions

1. Trace the teddy bear body (A) on the brown felt. Trace the circle (B) on the orange felt.

2. Cut out 2 brown teddy bear bodies. Cut out 3 orange circles. Cut or punch out 3 ¼-inch black dots.

3. Pin the 2 sides of the body together.

4. Paste the 2 black dots in place, as shown in the composite sketch on this page. Place 1 orange circle for the snout in place. Paste the other 2 orange circles on the bottom for the paws as shown. Paste 1 black dot in the center of the orange snout circle.

5. Sew the teddy bear all around, starting at the side, continuing around one arm, over the head, and down the other side. Leave a 3-inch opening.

6. Stuff with cotton, making sure it gets into the head and arms.

7. Finish by sewing up the opening and removing pins.

* For a complete bear family, see patterns on pages 34 and 66.

48

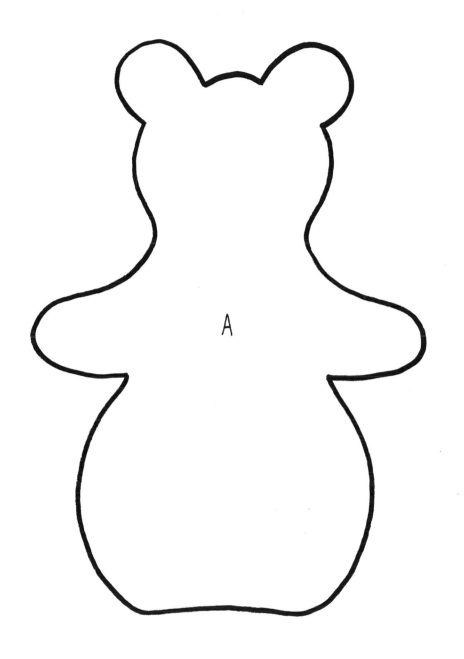

A

B

3. hand puppets

general instructions for making all hand puppets

1. All bodies are made from two 9 × 12-inch rectangles of the same color felt. For each design, "pieces of felt" refers to 9 × 12-inch rectangles. When the word "scrap" appears, it means that only a small piece of that particular color is needed. (You can judge the amount needed by the pattern requirement of that color for eyes, ears, noses, etc.) There is no pattern for ¼-inch eyes; simply punch them out with a hole puncher.

2. Trace the body outline of the pattern on one piece of felt. Then, making sure the two pieces of felt for the body are exactly aligned, cut out the two pieces at the same time. This makes sure that both sides match perfectly and you need only draw the pattern once.

3. Always use a large pair of scissors to cut out the body of the puppet—a smaller pair of scissors for the other parts.

4. Paste the small parts (eyes, nose, mouth, etc.) onto the body *before* sewing. Put the glue on the *small* part, not the body.

5. Pin or paste parts like ears and tails in place before sewing. Pin the two parts of the hand puppet together before sewing them.

6. The basic body designs for the hand puppets are found on pages 52-53 and 68-69.

7. Be sure to reinforce the corners where you insert a hand.

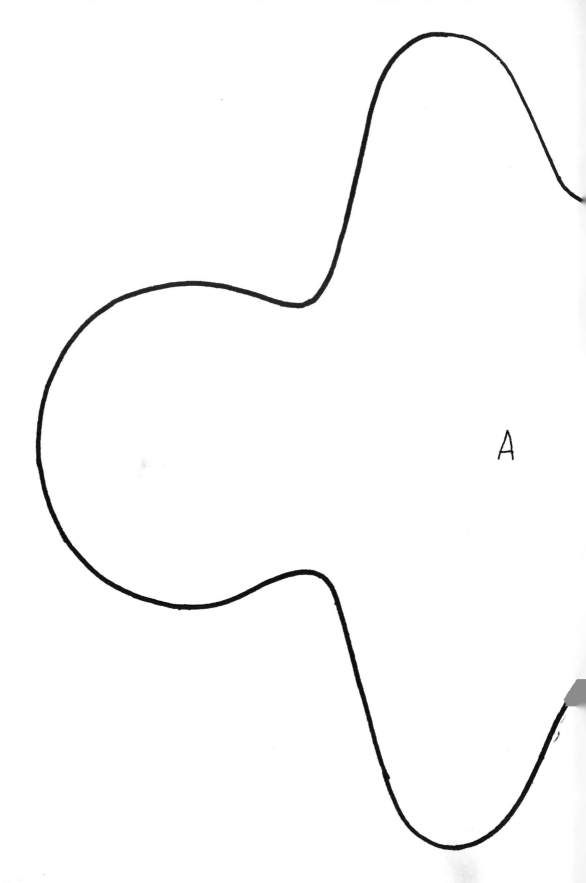

A

NOTE: This is the basic body outline for the following hand puppet patterns: Koala Bear (page 54), Owl (page 56), Clown (page 58), Snowman (page 60), Santa Claus (page 62), and Gingerbread Boy (page 64). The rest of the parts are found with the instructions for each puppet.

KOALA BEAR HAND PUPPET

materials needed

2 pieces of mustard-colored felt for the body
1 scrap each of black,
   white, red, and brown felt
   mustard-colored thread to match

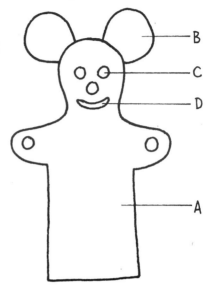

directions

1. Trace the koala bear body (A, found on pages 52-53) on the mustard-colored felt. Trace the ears (B) on the brown felt. Trace the mouth (D) on the red felt. Trace circles (C) on the black and white felt.

2. Cut out 2 mustard-colored bodies. Cut out 2 brown ears. Cut out 1 red mouth. Cut out 3 black circles and 2 white circles.

3. Pin the 2 sides of the puppet all around.

4. Trim the bottom edge with pinking shears.

5. Paste the ears between the two body layers at the top of the head, as shown in the composite diagram on this page. Paste the circles for eyes, nose, and paws on the body, as shown (the eyes and nose are the black circles, the paws are white). Paste the mouth in position.

6. Sew the hand puppet all around, starting at the bottom corner of the pinked edge (do not sew around the outer edge of the ears). Leave the bottom pinked edge open to insert hand.

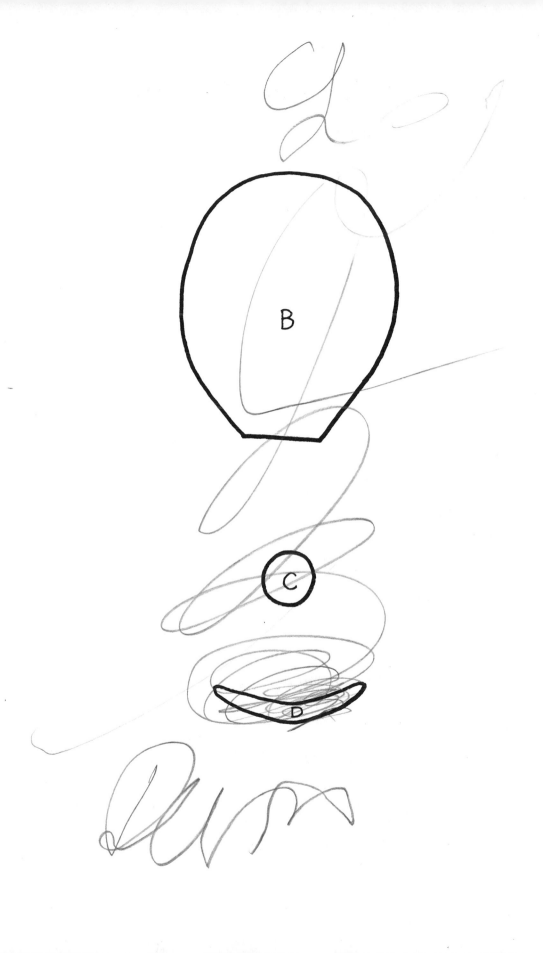

OWL HAND PUPPET

materials needed

2 pieces of dark gray felt for the body
1 scrap each of yellow,
　　white, and black felt
　　gray thread to match

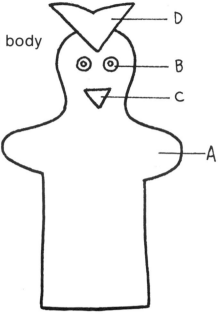

directions

1. Trace the owl body (A, found on pages 52-53) on the gray felt. Trace the outline of the large triangle (D) and the small triangle (C) on the yellow felt. Trace the outline of the circle (B) on the white felt.

2. Cut out the 2 gray owl bodies. Cut out 1 small yellow triangle. Cut out the large yellow triangle with pinking shears, if you have them. Cut out 2 white circles. Cut or punch out 2 ¼-inch black dots for the eyes.

3. Pin the 2 sides of the puppet together.

4. Trim the bottom edge with pinking shears, if available.

5. Paste the large yellow triangle in the center of the head so that the wing-like parts stick up, as shown in the composite diagram on this page. Paste the 2 white circles in place. Paste the small yellow triangle in place for the nose. Paste the 2 black dots on the white circles for the eyes.

6. Sew the hand puppet all around, starting at the bottom corner of the pinked edge, going up one side and down the other. Leave the bottom pinked edge open to insert hand.

CLOWN HAND PUPPET

terials needed

ces of pink felt for the body
ap each of black,
white, red, yellow,
and blue felt
k thread to match

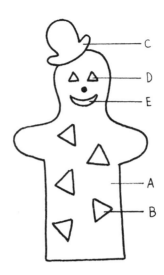

ections

ace the clown body (A, found on pages 52-53) on the
felt. Trace the large triangle (B) on the black, white, red,
w, and blue felt. Trace the small triangle (D) on the black
Trace the mouth (E) on the red felt. Trace the hat (C) on
lue felt.

it out the 2 pink body outlines. Cut out 1 large triangle
ch color. Cut out 2 small black triangles. Cut out 1 red
th and 2 blue hats. Cut or punch out 1 white ¼-inch dot
ie nose.

n the 2 sides of the puppet together.

im the bottom edge with pinking shears, if available.

iste the 2 small black triangles on the face for eyes, as
vn in the composite diagram on this page. Paste the nose
mouth in place. Paste the large triangles around the
in an uneven pattern.

ew the hand puppet all around, starting at the bottom
er of the pinked edge, going up one side and down the
nd side. Leave the bottom pinked edge open to
t hand.

iste the top of the 2 hat parts together, making sure
sides match perfectly and leaving the brim open for the
ient. Now, paste the brim on the front and back of the
, as shown.

SNOWMAN HAND PUPPET

materials needed

2 pieces of white felt for the body
1 scrap each of red and black felt
    white thread to match

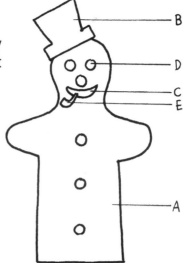

directions

1. Trace the snowman body (A, found on pages 52-53) on the white felt. Trace the hat (B) and pipe (E) on the black felt. Trace the mouth (C) on the red felt. Trace the ½-inch circle (D) on the red and black felt.

2. Cut out 2 white body outlines. Cut out 2 hats, 1 pipe, and 3 circles in black. Cut out the mouth and 3 more circles in red.

3. Pin the 2 sides of the puppet together.

4. Trim the bottom edge with pinking shears, if available.

5. Paste 2 black circles in place for the eyes, as shown in the composite diagram on this page. Paste 1 red circle in place for the nose. Paste the pipe on the face as shown. Allow it to dry and then paste the mouth over the top of the pipe as shown. For buttons paste the remaining 3 circles down the front of the snowman evenly—red, then black, then red.

6. Sew the hand puppet all around, starting at the bottom corner of the pinked edge, going up one side and down the other. Leave the bottom pinked edge open to insert hand.

7. Paste the top of the 2 hat parts together, making sure both sides match perfectly, and leaving the brim open for the moment. Now, paste the brim on the front and back of the head, as shown.

60

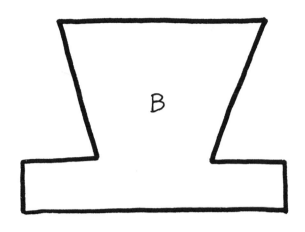

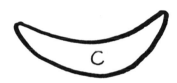

SANTA CLAUS HAND PUPPET

materials needed

2 pieces of red felt for the body and hat
1 scrap each of white and black felt
   red thread to match

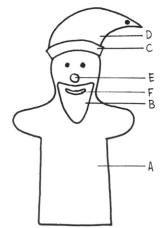

directions

1. Trace the Santa Claus body (A, found on pages 52-53) on the red felt. Trace the hat (D) on the red felt. Trace the outline of the beard (B), hatband (C), and ½-inch circle (E) on the white felt. Trace the mouth (F) on black felt. Trace the circle (E) again on black felt.

2. Cut out 2 red Santa Claus bodies and 2 red hats. Cut out 1 white beard (with pinking shears, if available) and 1 white circle. Cut out the black mouth and 3 black circles. Cut or punch out 2 black ¼-inch dots and 1 white ¼-inch dot.

3. Pin the 2 sides of the puppet together.

4. Trim the bottom edge with pinking shears, if available.

5. Paste the 2 black eye circles in place, as shown in the composite diagram on this page. Paste the beard and nose (½-inch white circle) in place, as shown. For buttons paste the 3 black circles in place. Paste the mouth over the beard. Paste the top 2 hat parts together, making sure both sides match and leaving the brim open for the moment. Now, paste the brim onto the front and back of the head, as shown. Paste the white ¼-inch dot on the tip of the hat.

6. Sew the hand puppet all around, starting at the bottom corner of the pinked edge, going up one side and down the other. Leave the bottom pinked edge open to insert hand.

7. Paste the hatband (C) across bottom of hat so that it lines up with sides.

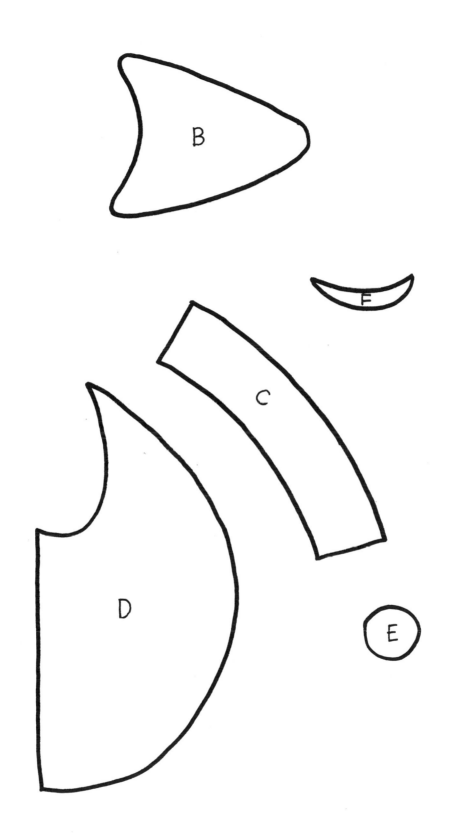

B

F

C

D

E

GINGERBREAD BOY
HAND PUPPET

materials needed

2 pieces of brown felt for the body
1 scrap each of orange, red,
    white, and black felt
  white thread

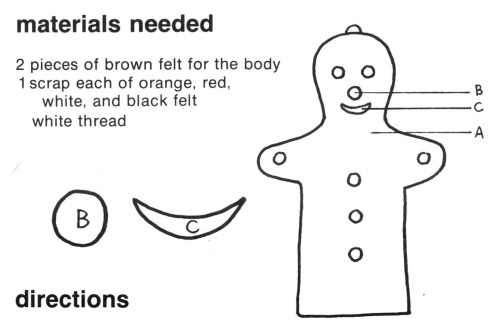

directions

1. Trace the gingerbread boy body (A, found on pages 52-53) on the brown felt. Trace the circle (B) on the black, orange, white, and red felt. Trace the mouth (C) on the red felt.

2. Cut out 2 brown gingerbread boy bodies. Cut out 3 orange circles, 4 black circles, and 1 each of red and white. Cut out the mouth.

3. Pin the 2 sides of the puppet together.

4. Trim the bottom edge with pinking shears.

5. Paste the red circle at the top of the head, half way in, between the 2 layers of the head. Paste the other circles on the body, as shown in the composite diagram on this page. Use black for the eyes and paws, white for the nose and hands, orange for the buttons. Paste the mouth in position.

6. Sew the hand puppet all around, but leave the bottom pinked edge open to insert hand.

LEOPARD HAND PUPPET

materials needed

2 pieces of orange felt for the body
1 scrap each of black, white, and red felt
   orange thread to match

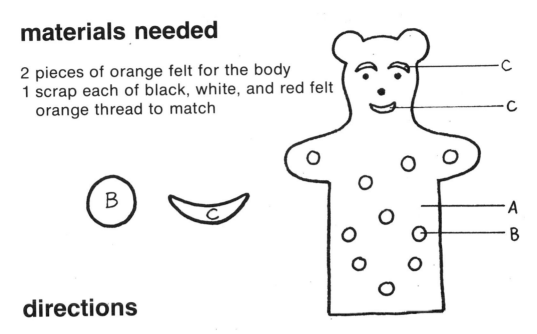

directions

1. Trace the leopard body (A, found on pages 68-69) on the orange felt. Trace the ½-inch circle (B) on the black, white, and red felt. Trace the outline of the eyebrow (C) on the black felt.

2. Cut out 2 orange leopard bodies. Cut out 4 black circles, 3 white circles, and 3 red circles. Cut out 3 black eyebrows (one will be the mouth when turned upside down). Cut or punch out 2 black ¼-inch dots for eyes and 1 white ¼-inch dot for the nose.

3. Pin the 2 sides of the puppet together.

4. Trim the bottom edge with pinking shears.

5. Paste the 2 black eyebrows in place, as shown in the composite diagram on this page. Paste a ¼-inch black dot (eye) under each eyebrow, as shown. Paste the white ¼-inch dot (nose) in place. Paste the mouth (upside-down eyebrow) in place. Paste the black, white, and red ½-inch circles on the body in a scattered pattern as pictured.

6. Sew the hand puppet all around, starting at the bottom corner of the pinked edge, going up one side and down the other. Leave the bottom pinked edge open to insert hand.

TEDDY BEAR HAND PUPPET
(papa bear*)

materials needed

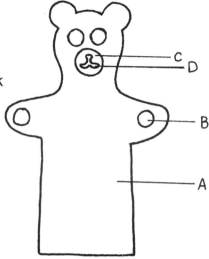

2 pieces of brown felt for the body
   scraps of yellow, white, and black
      felt for the eyes,
        nose-mouth, and paws
   brown thread to match

directions

1. Trace the teddy bear body (A, found on pages 68-69) on the brown felt. Trace the ½-inch circle (B) on the yellow and white felt. Trace the 1-inch circle (C) on the yellow felt. Trace the nose-mouth (D) on the black felt.

2. Cut out 2 brown bear bodies. Cut out 4 yellow ½-inch circles and 1 yellow 1-inch circle. Cut out 2 white ½-inch circles. Cut out the nose-mouth in black. Cut or punch out 2 ¼-inch black dots for the eyes.

3. Pin the 2 sides of the puppet all around.

4. Trim the bottom edge with pinking shears.

5. Paste the 2 "whites" of the eyes (½-inch circles) in place, as shown in the composite diagram on this page. Let dry. Paste the 1-inch yellow circle that goes under the nose-mouth in place, as shown. Paste the 2 yellow circles on each paw. Now, paste each black dot in the center of the white eye circles. Paste the nose-mouth over the yellow circle, as shown.

6. Sew the hand puppet all around, starting at the bottom corner of the pinked edge, going up one side and down the other. Leave the bottom pinked edge open to insert hand.

* For a complete bear family, see patterns on pages 34 and 48.

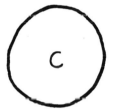

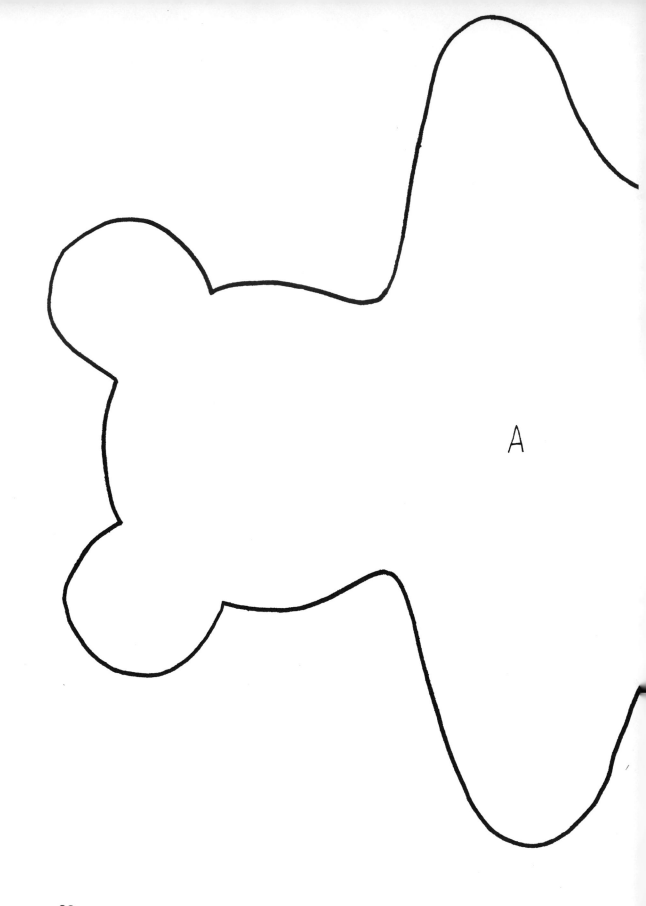

A

NOTE: This is the basic body outline for the following hand puppet patterns: Leopard (page 65), and Teddy Bear (page 66).

4. hangers and mobiles

general instructions for covering hangers

materials needed

1 inexpensive wooden dress hanger any size
1 piece of 9 × 12-inch felt, any color you choose (make it
    match or blend with the rest of the hanger decoration)
  thread to match the felt

directions

1. Measure the hanger from the center to one end.

2. Cut out 2 lengths of felt that are long enough to cover
each half of the hanger bar from the hook to the end and
wide enough to go around the circumference of the hanger.

3. Wrapping one length of felt around one half of the hanger
bar, sew it together over the bar. Using an overcast stitch, start
at the hook, sew the length of the bar, and close up the end.

4. Repeat for the other half of the hanger.

5. Now, slip off each felt cover and turn inside out (take
a pointless pencil or any similar object, poke it against the
closed end, and roll the felt covering over it until covering
is inside out with the stitches on the inside).

6. Slip the covers over the hanger so that they meet at the
center where the hook is. Keep the stitches at the bottom
of the hanger.

7. Now, by hand, sew the 2 sides of the felt covers together
where they meet at the hook.

8. Cut a small piece of felt about 1 inch wide and the
circumference of the hanger (use the same or a contrasting
color).

9. Paste the felt over the seam in the center of the hanger.

10. Hanger is now ready for decorative designs shown on
following pages.

CHICKEN HANGER

materials needed

1 felt-covered hanger (see general directions on page 71)
1 piece of yellow felt (makes 4 chickens)
1 scrap each of orange and black felt
    cotton for stuffing
    yellow thread to match

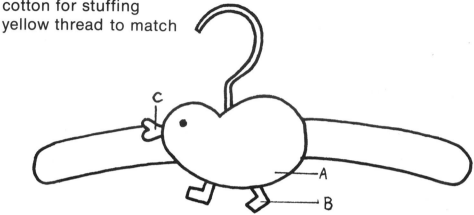

directions

1. Trace the chicken body (A) on the yellow felt. Trace the beak (C) and the feet (B) on the orange felt.

2. Cut out 2 yellow chicken bodies. Cut out 2 feet and 1 beak. Cut or punch out a ¼-inch black dot for the eye.

3. Pin the 2 sides of the chicken together.

4. Paste the beak between the 2 parts of the chicken, as shown in the composite diagram on this page. Paste the feet between the 2 parts of the body, as shown. Paste the eye in place.

5. Sew the chicken all around, starting at the top of the beak, and going around the beak and feet and up the other side. Leave a 3-inch opening at the top.

6. Stuff a small amount of cotton into the opening.

7. Finish by sewing up the opening and removing pins.

8. Now, sew the back side of the finished chicken to the center of the felt-covered hanger. Use large tacking stitches to secure it.

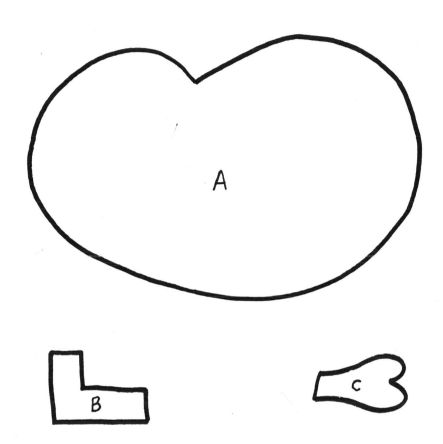

A

B

C

MOUSE HANGER

materials needed

1 felt-covered hanger (see general instructions on p. 71)
1 piece of yellow felt (makes 4 mice)
1 scrap of red felt
1 ¼-inch sequin
   cotton for stuffing
   yellow thread to match

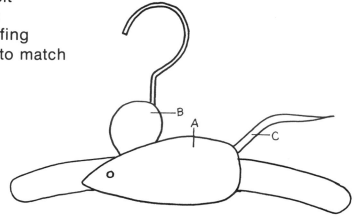

directions

1. Trace the mouse body (A) on the yellow felt. Trace the outline of the ear (B) and tail (C) on the red felt.

2. Cut out 2 yellow mouse bodies. Cut out 1 red ear and 1 red tail.

3. Pin the 2 sides of the mouse together.

4. Paste the ear between the 2 sides of the body at the top as shown in the composite diagram on this page. Paste the tail between the two sides, as shown. Paste the sequin in place for an eye.

5. Sew the mouse all around, starting at the nose and continuing around the ear and tail to the bottom. Leave a 3-inch opening.

6. Stuff a small amount of cotton into the opening.

7. Finish by sewing up the opening and removing the pins.

8. Sew the back side of finished mouse to the center of the felt-covered hanger. Use large tacking stitches.

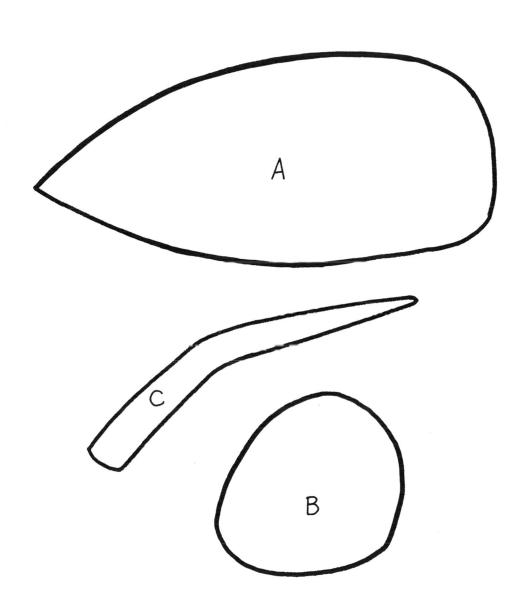

BUTTERFLY HANGER

materials needed

1 felt-covered hanger (see general directions on page 71)
1 piece of pink felt (makes 4 butterflies)
1 scrap each of brown and white felt
6 ¼-inch colored sequins
   cotton for stuffing
   pink thread to match

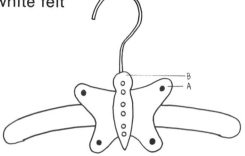

directions

1. Trace the outline of the butterfly wings (A) on the pink felt. Trace the outline of the body (B) on the brown felt.

2. Cut out 2 pink wing parts. Cut out 2 brown body parts. Cut or punch out 4 white ¼-inch dots.

3. Pin the 2 sides of the wings together.

4. Sew the wings together, starting at the top corner of one wing and continuing all around to the top corner of the other wing. Leave the top (where the head will be) open.

5. Paste 1 white dot at the corner of each wing as shown.

6. Stuff a small amount of cotton into the opening.

7. Sew up the opening (use a running stitch if sewing by hand).

8. Paste the 6 sequins down the front of 1 brown body part.

9. Paste the *undecorated* brown body part down the center of the *undecorated* stuffed wing part. Leave head and tail free, as shown in the composite diagram on this page.

10. Now, paste the *sequined* brown body part down the center of the *decorated* stuffed wing part. Paste the heads and tails together so they match exactly.

11. Sew the back side of finished butterfly to the center of the felt-covered hanger, using large tacking stitches.

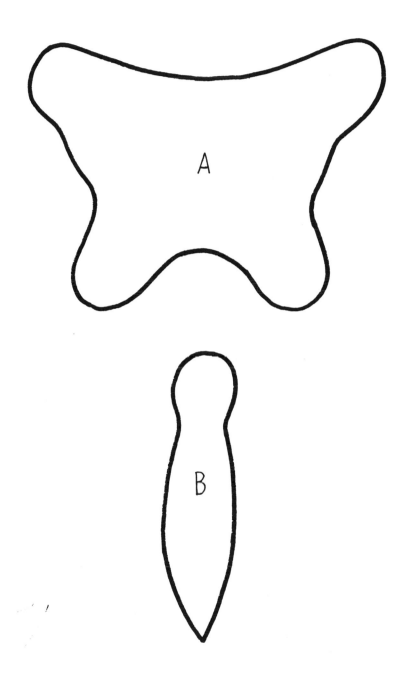

A

B

SOLDIER HANGER

materials needed

1 felt-covered hanger (see general directions on page 71)
1 piece of green felt
1 piece of white felt (makes 2 soldiers)
  scrap of red felt
6 sequins
  cotton for stuffing
  white thread

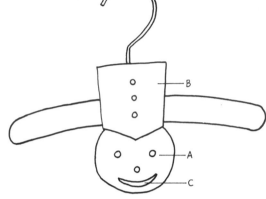

directions

1. Trace the soldier's face (A) on the white felt. Trace the hat (B) on the green felt. Trace the mouth (C) on the red felt.

2. Cut out 2 white faces, 2 green hats, and 1 red mouth.

3. Pin the 2 sides of the face together. Pin the 2 sides of the hat together.

4. Paste the sequins in place on the face for the eyes and nose, as shown in the composite diagram on this page. Paste the mouth in place. Paste the 3 sequins down the center of the hat, as shown.

5. Sew the face ¾ of the way around, leaving the top open. Sew the hat together around its 3 straight edges, leaving the pointed part open. Use a running stitch for both face and hat.

6. Stuff the face with enough cotton so that it sticks up and will stuff the hat, too. Now, place the hat over the cotton and about 1 inch over the top of the face. Do *not* sew up the face opening.

7. Stitch the front and back of the hat to the face.

8. Sew the back soldier's head to the center of the hanger, using large tacking stitches.

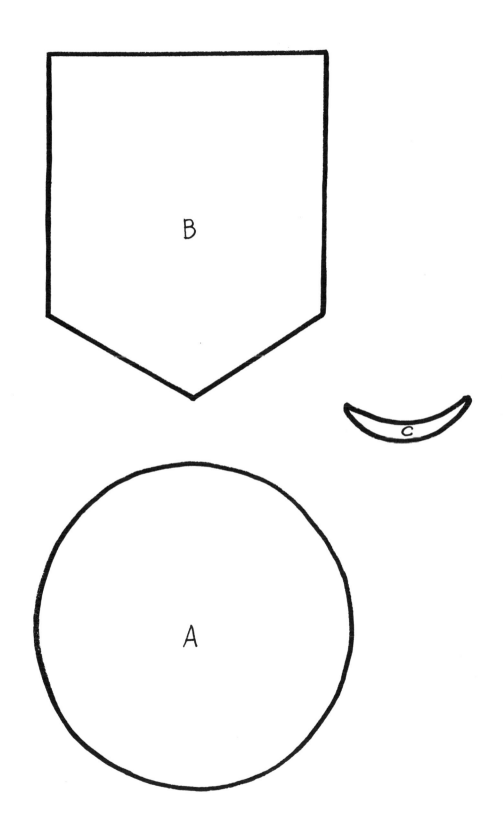

B

C

A

KITE MOBILE

materials needed

1 large scrap of royal blue felt
1 small scrap of red felt
   royal blue thread to match

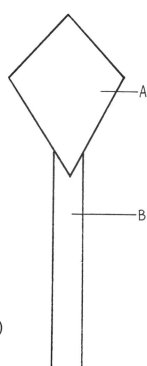

directions

1. Trace the outline of the kite (A) on the blue felt. Trace the tail (B) on the red felt.

2. Cut out 2 blue kites. Cut out 1 red tail (with pinking shears) if available.

3. Paste 1 end of the red tail on the longest corner of one blue kite, placing the tail in about ¼ inch. Now, paste the 2 blue kites together so that the tail is on the inside.

4. Thread a needle with royal blue thread and run it through the top of the kite about ⅛ inch from the edge.

5. Tie a knot in the thread at the top of the kite and cut off loose end of thread.

6. Leave a length of thread as long as you want and make a loop at the other end. Hang mobile from a cup screw in the wall or ceiling or from a light fixture.

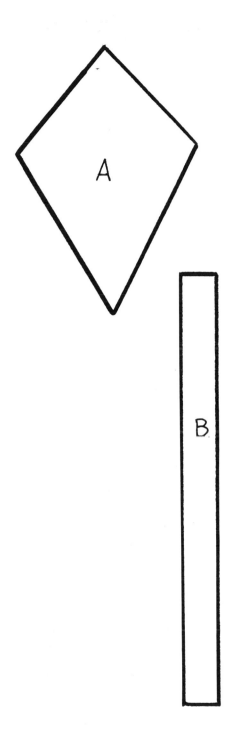

FISH MOBILE

materials needed

1 piece of yellow felt (makes 4 mobiles)
1 scrap of royal blue felt
8 colored sequins
   royal blue thread to match

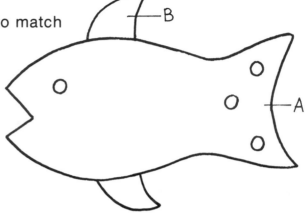

directions

1. Trace the fish body (A) on the yellow felt. Trace the outline of the fin (B) on the blue felt.

2. Cut out 2 yellow fish. Cut out 2 blue fins.

3. Paste 1 fin at the top of the fish body, as shown in the composite diagram on this page. About ¼ inch of the straight edge of the fin should be pasted to the fish body. Paste the other fin at the bottom of the fish in the same manner. Now paste the 2 fish bodies together so they meet exactly. Allow to dry.

4. Paste a colored sequin in place for the eye. Paste 3 colored sequins on the tail, as shown in the composite diagram on this page. Repeat on the other side using the same color sequins in the same spots.

5. Thread a needle with royal blue thread. Put the needle through the top fin about ⅛ inch from the top point.

6. Tie a knot in the thread at the top of the fin and cut off loose end of thread.

7. Leave a length of thread as long as you want and make a loop at the other end. Hang mobile from the wall or ceiling or hook onto a light fixture.

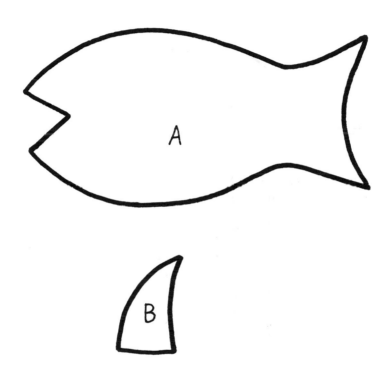

A

B

SAILBOAT MOBILE

materials needed

1 large scrap of white felt
1 scrap each of blue and red felt
   white thread

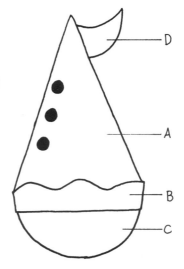

directions

1. Trace the outline of the sail (A) on the white felt. Trace the outline of the boat (C) on the blue felt. Trace the flag (D) and the curvy "deck" (B) on the red felt.

2. Cut out 2 white sails. Cut out 1 blue boat. Cut out 1 red flag and 2 red decks. Cut or punch out 6 red dots, ¼ inch each.

3. Paste the blue boat part between the bottom of the 2 white sails—inserting the straight part of the boat about ½ inch. Allow to dry. Paste the flag between the sails at the top, as shown in the composite diagram on this page. Insert the straight end of the flag in about ¼ inch. Now paste on a red deck where the sail and boat meet. Repeat on the other side. Paste the white sails together so they meet exactly. Trim off any uneven edges. Finally, paste 3 red ¼-inch dots down one side of the sail, as shown. Do the same on the other sail, placing the dots in the same position.

4. Thread a needle with white thread and put it through the top of the sails about ⅛ inch from the edge.

5. Tie a knot in the thread at the top of the sails and cut off loose end of thread.

6. Leave a length of thread as long as you want and make a loop at the other end. Hang mobile from a wall, ceiling, or light fixture.

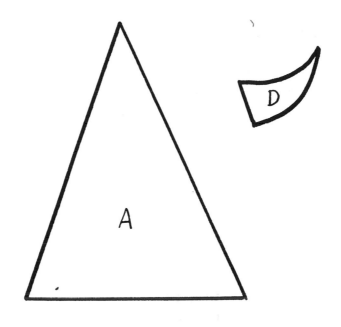

A

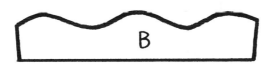

B

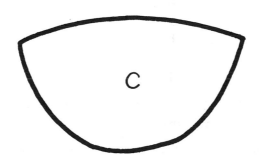

C

D

PIG MOBILE

materials needed

1 large scrap of pink felt
1 small scrap of light blue, black, white, and red felt
   pink thread to match

directions

1. Trace the outline of the pig (A) on the pink felt. Trace the ears (B) and feet (also B) on the blue felt. Trace the outline of the circle (C) on the white felt. Trace the outline of the mouth (D) on the red felt.

2. Cut out 2 pink pig bodies. Cut out 4 ears and 2 feet in blue. Cut out 2 white circles. Cut out 2 red mouths. Also cut or punch out 4 black ¼-inch dots for eyes.

3. Paste the two feet—narrow end inside—at the bottom of one of the pink circles, inserting them about ¼ inch and about 1½ inches apart, as indicated in the composite diagram on this page. Now, paste the two pink circles together so they match up evenly. Paste the blue ears, black eyes, white nose, and red mouth in place, as shown.

4. With a black laundry marker or fine felt pen, ink in 2 dots on the white nose for nostrils.

5. Paste the ears, eyes, nose, and mouth in place on the other (blank) side of the pink circle in exactly the same spots so that the pig is two-faced.

6. Thread a needle with pink thread and put it through the head about ⅛ inch from the top.

7. Tie a knot in the thread at the top of the head and cut off loose end.

8. Leave a length of thread as long as you want and hang mobile from wall, ceiling, or light fixture.

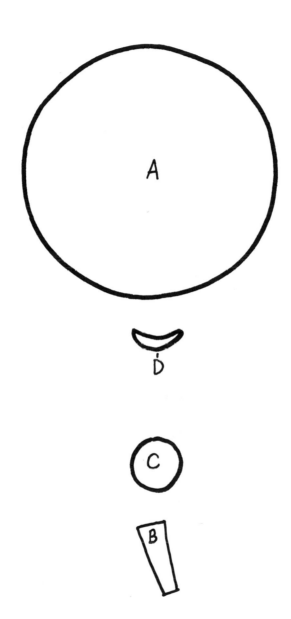

CLOWN MOBILE

materials needed

1 large scrap of white felt
1 large scrap of blue felt
1 scrap each of red, black,
    pink, and orange felt
orange thread to match

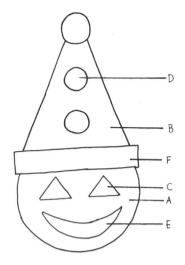

directions

1. Trace the face (A) on the white felt. Trace hat (B) on the blue felt. Trace the hat ruffle (F) on the pink felt. Trace the mouth (E) on the red felt. Trace the small triangle (C) on the black felt. Trace the small circle (D) on the red and orange felt.

2. Cut out 2 large white circles, 2 large blue triangles, 2 pink hat ruffles, 2 red mouths, 4 small black triangles, 4 small red circles, and 2 small orange circles.

3. Paste the 2 white faces together. Paste 1 blue hat triangle at the top of the face about 1 inch down from the top. Now, paste the other blue triangle hat on the other side in the same spot and press the 2 sides together so that they match up evenly. Paste a pink hat ruffle where the hat and face meet, 1 on each side. Paste 2 red circles down the center of each hat, 2 on each side. Paste the 2 orange circles together over the point of the hat. Paste the small black triangles in place for the eyes, 2 on each side. Paste a mouth in place on each side of the face.

4. Thread a needle with orange thread and put it through the top of the orange circles.

5. Tie a knot in the thread and cut off loose end.

6. Leave a length of thread as long as you want and make a loop at the other end. Hang mobile from a cup screw or ceiling or light fixture.

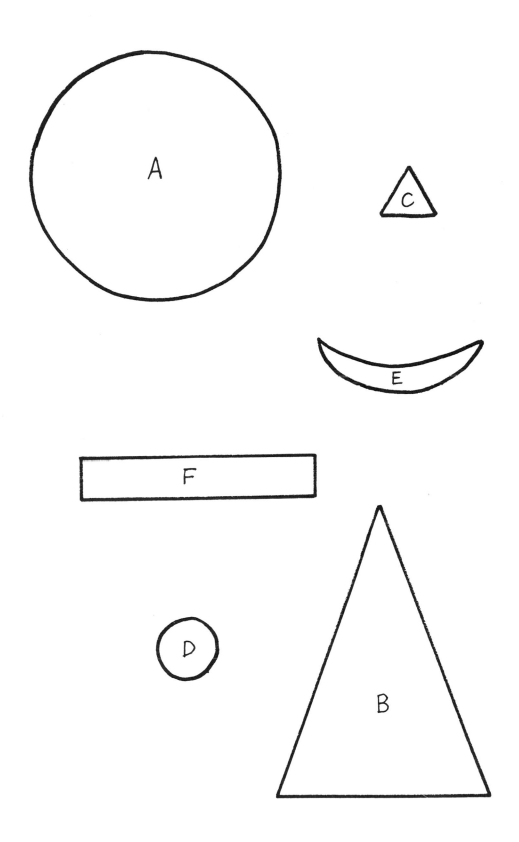

5. bookmarks

general directions for making bookmarks

Bookmarks are great for the youngsters to make because there is no sewing, nor is absolute accuracy required.

1. Any scrap of felt that measures ½ inch wide and 6 to 9 inches long can be used for the bookmark. Any other scrap of a different color can be used for the decoration.

2. Pinking shears are not essential for cutting out the bookmarks, but they do give the finished product a more professional look. Besides, if the youngster is cutting out the bookmark, a little wrong snip or curve here or there won't show as much when the edges are pinked.

3. The bookmark itself should be only 1 thickness of felt. The main portion of the designs should always be cut out in 2 pieces and pasted together on either side of the bookmark to give them more body. Any small parts of the design such as leaves or ¼-inch dots should be only 1 thickness or 1 piece of felt.

4. The outline of the bookmark remains the same except you may vary the length, if you like.

5. The directions for making a tulip bookmark appear on the following page. With these same instructions, use any of the designs for clipboards and bookmarks (they can be used for both) to make any other bookmark you desire. Try making a clipboard and bookmark to match, using the same design for both.

6. See page 94 for more patterns and composite diagrams of bookmarks.

TULIP BOOKMARK

materials needed

1 scrap of green felt about 1 inch wide and 6 to 9 inches long
1 scrap of red felt

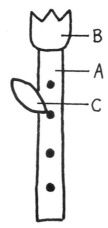

directions

1. Trace the outline of the bookmark (A) on the green felt. Trace the tulip (B) on the red felt. Trace the leaf (C) on the green felt.

2. Cut out the bookmark with pinking shears, if available, or straight scissors so that it ends up about ½ inch to ¾ inch wide and as long as you wish. Cut out 2 red tulips and 1 green leaf. Cut or punch out 4 red ¼-inch dots.

3. Paste 1 end of the bookmark on 1 red tulip, placing the end of the bookmark over the tulip about ¼ inch. Now, paste the 2 tulips together so they match up perfectly, with the bookmark between the 2 parts.

4. Paste the 4 red dots down the center of the bookmark, spacing them evenly, as shown in the composite diagram on this page. Finally, paste the green leaf just above the second red dot, as shown.

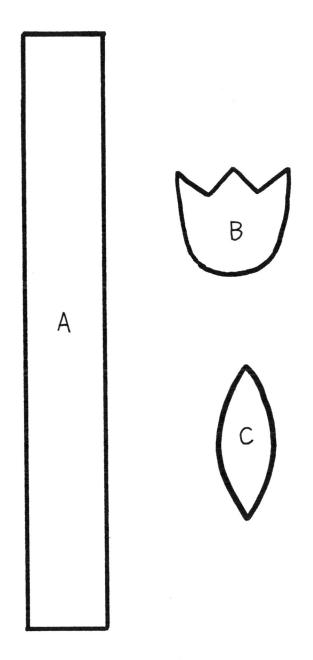

A

B

C

more bookmarks to make

Here are 5 more bookmark patterns, all of which can easily be made according to the instructions on page 91.

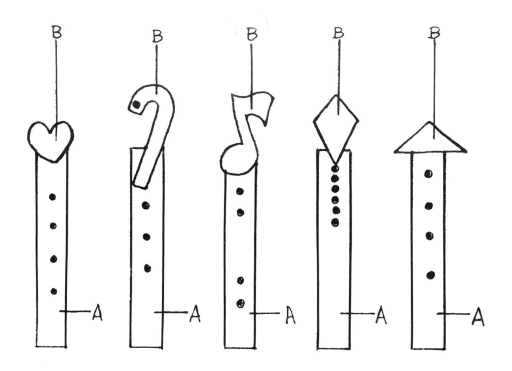

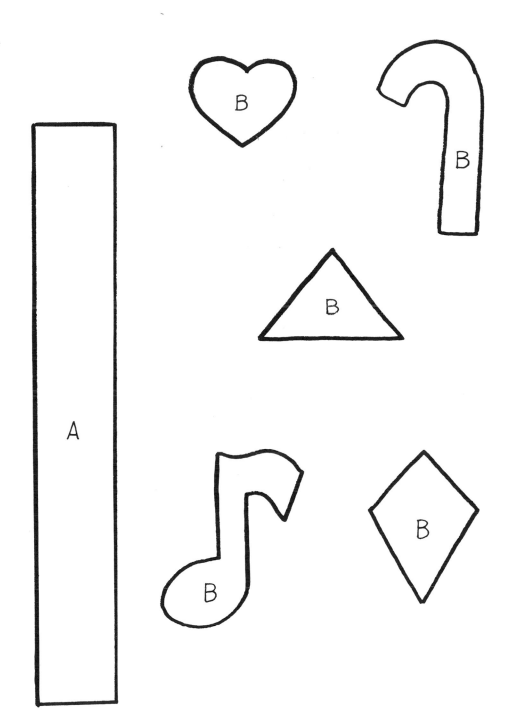

6. clipboards

general directions for making clipboards

1. The backing for the clipboards can be any heavy, thick piece of cardboard. The best backing to use is double-ply mat board, which can be purchased in any art-supply store and in some stationery stores. It usually comes in large sheets of about 20 x 36-inches. It you wish, the salesman in the store will cut the sheet into equal parts. First, decide what size you want to make the clipboards. The directions that follow are for one 9 x 12-inch clipboard and one 8 x 6-inch clipboard. You may use any size you wish.

2. When gluing the felt to the board, put the glue on the *board,* not on the felt. Use a very thin layer of glue and even it out with your finger or a thin brush.

3. When you place the felt over the glued surface, smooth out the wrinkles. If there is any overlap, cut off the edges with a straight pair of scissors so that the felt and the board are exactly even.

4. Let the felt dry thoroughly before pasting on the decorations.

5. Always lay out the decorations on the felt-covered board before pasting them on, to make sure the decorations are evenly spaced.

6. Use any of the illustrated designs to decorate the clipboards. The designs for clipboards and bookmarks are interchangeable. The smaller designs will fit the smaller boards better than the larger ones.

7. The clip for the board is called a bulldog letter clip and can be purchased in most five-and-dime stores or stationery stores, as can the pads of paper for the clipboard.

8. The directions for making a high boot clipboard and a mushroom clipboard follow on the next 2 pages. Since the bookmark designs are interchangeable with those for clipboards, see pages 94-95 for more designs.

HIGH BOOT CLIPBOARD

materials needed

1 8 x 6-inch double-ply mat board
1 8 x 6-inch piece of royal blue felt
1 large scrap of pink felt
1 small scrap of black felt
1 bulldog letter clip
1 3½ x 6-inch pad of paper

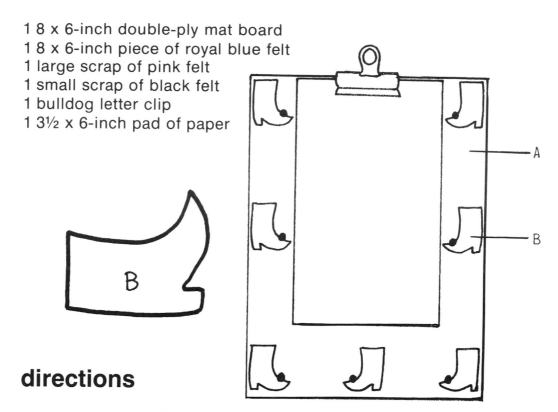

directions

1. Cover the board with a thin layer of glue.
2. Place the piece of blue felt (A) on the glue-covered surface. Smooth out the wrinkles. Trim off any overlap. Allow to dry.

3. Outline the boot design (B) on the pink felt.

4. Cut out 7 pink felt boots. Cut or punch out 7 ¼-inch black dots.

5. Paste the boots down the sides of the felt-covered board, as shown in the composite diagram on this page. Paste the heel part of the boot on the outer edge with the toe pointing inward. Paste 1 pink boot in the middle of the board at the bottom (point that boot in either direction). Paste 1 black dot on the toe of each boot, as shown.

6. Place the blank pad of paper in the center of the clipboard and secure it at the top with the letter clip.

MUSHROOM CLIPBOARD

materials needed

1 9 x 12-inch double-ply mat board
1 9 x 12-inch piece of pink felt
1 large scrap each of red and white felt
1 bulldog letter clip
1 5 x 8-inch pad of paper

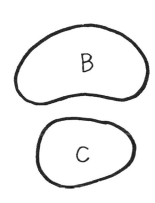

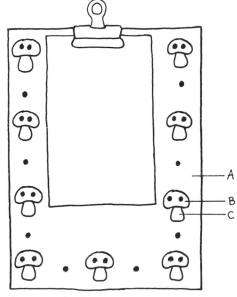

directions

1. Cover the board with a thin layer of glue.

2. Place the piece of pink felt (A) on top of the glue-covered surface. Smooth out the wrinkles. Trim off any overlap. Allow to dry.

3. Outline the top of the mushroom (B) on the red felt. Outline the stem of the mushroom (C) on the white felt.

4. Cut out 9 red mushroom tops and 9 white mushroom stems. Cut or punch out 26 white ¼-inch dots.

5. Paste 4 mushroom stems down each side of the felt-covered board, evenly spaced, as shown in the composite diagram on this page. Paste a stem in the center at the bottom of the board. Now, paste a red mushroom top over the top of each white stem. Paste a white dot on each corner of the red tops. Paste another white dot between each completed mushroom.

6. Place the blank pad in the center of the clipboard and secure it at the top with the letter clip.

7. practical and pretty

KEY-CHAIN HOLDER

materials needed

1 scrap of red felt (use scraps from eyeglass cases on
previous page to make 3 key-chain holders)
1 scrap of pink felt for two hearts
1 dime-store key chain

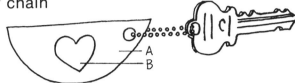

directions

1. Trace the pattern for the key-chain holder (A) on the red felt. Trace the heart pattern (B) on the pink felt.

2. Cut out 2 red key-chain holders with pinking shears, if available. Cut out 2 pink hearts with straight scissors.

3. Pin the 2 sides of the key-chain holder together.

4. Sew the key-chain holder all around, using a running stitch. Stay as close to the edge of the material as possible.

5. Paste 1 red heart on each side of the key-chain holder.

6. Punch a ¼-inch hole through both thicknesses of felt about ¼ inch in from the edge of the material, being careful not to punch through the stitches.

7. Put the key chain through the hole. Now put your keys on the chain.

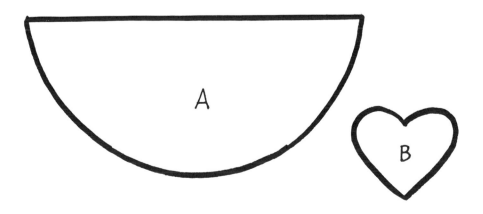

EYEGLASS CASE

materials needed

2 pieces of red felt (makes 3 eyeglass cases. Use scraps to
     make 3 matching key-chain holders)
1 scrap of pink felt for 6 hearts
   red thread to match

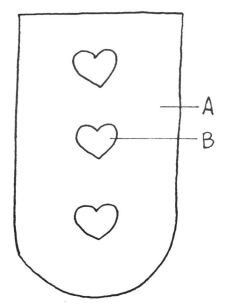

directions

1. Trace the pattern of the eyeglass case (A) on the red felt.
Trace the outline of the heart (B) on the pink felt.

2. Cut out 2 red eyeglass cases with pinking shears, if
available. Cut out 6 pink hearts with straight scissors.

3. Pin the 2 sides of the eyeglass case together.

4. Sew the two parts of the eyeglass case together on 3 sides,
leaving the top edges open to insert glasses. The glasses will
slip into the case and rest on the bottom, rounded surface.
Sew as close to the edge of the material as possible, using a
running stitch.

5. Paste 3 red hearts on each side of the case, as shown in
the composte diagram on this page.

6. Finished eyeglass case will hold any regular-size
glasses.

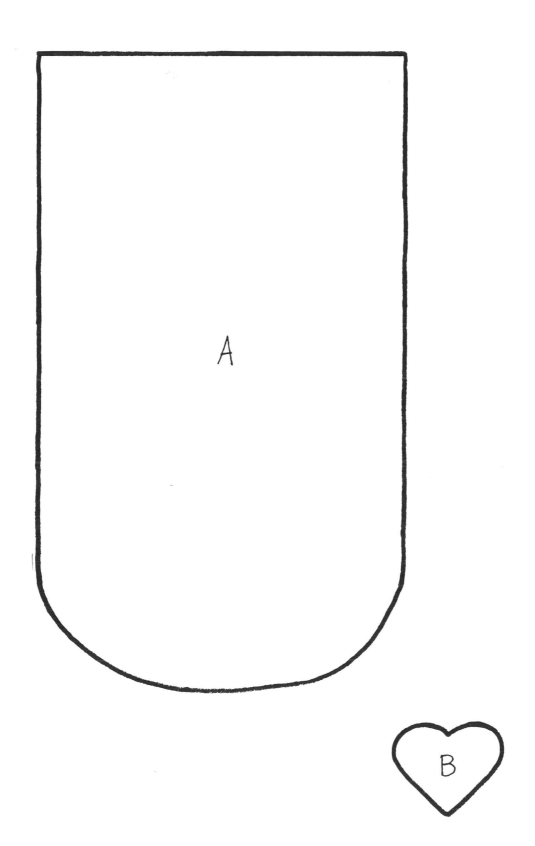

DRESSER OR PURSE MIRROR

materials needed

1 small round mirror with handle (about 3 inches in
    diameter)
1 scrap of yellow felt about 3¼ inches in diameter
1 scrap each of red felt and black felt
    enough 4-ply pink yarn to make 9 12-inch lengths and 2
    bows
1 small sequin (optional)

directions

1. Trace the outline of your mirror on one piece of yellow
felt. Trace the outline of the eyes (B) on the black felt and
the mouth (C) on the red felt.

2. Cut out all the parts.

3. Paste the round piece of yellow felt on the back of the
mirror.

4. Fringe the black eyes at the straight edge so they look like
eyelashes, as shown in the composite diagram on this page.
Now, paste the *oval* part of the eye on the yellow felt as shown,
leaving the lashes unpasted. Paste the mouth in place. Paste a
sequin "beauty spot" under one eye.

5. Cut the yarn into 9 12-inch strands. Make a braid using 3
strands of yarn for each of the 3 parts of the braid.

6. Tie the ends of the braid with a yarn bow. Trim ends
evenly.

7. Put a thin layer of glue all over one side of the braid
(except on loose ends) and press the braid firmly around the
outer edge of the face. Mirror is complete and ready for
dresser or purse.

8. See page 108 for matching comb case.

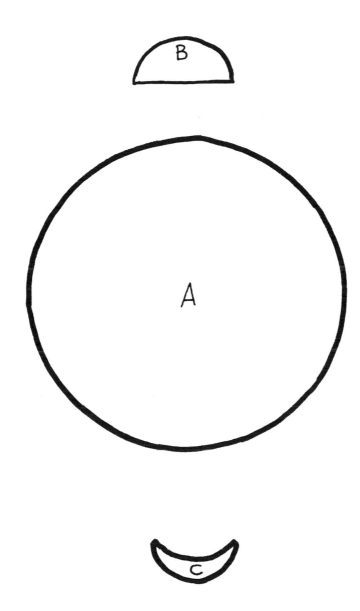

COMB CASE

(to match mirror on page 106)

materials needed

1 piece of yellow felt (makes 3 comb cases)
1 scrap of pink felt for decorations
   yellow thread to match
6 sequins (optional)
1 small pocket comb

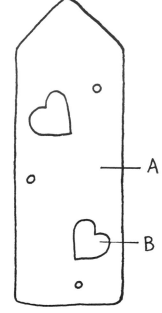

directions

1. Trace the outline of the comb case (A) on the yellow felt. Trace the heart (B) on the pink felt.

2. Cut out 2 yellow cases. Cut out 4 hearts.

3. Pink the top (pointed) edge of the comb case with pinking shears.

4. Pin both sides together.

5. Paste the hearts and sequins on both sides of the case, as shown in the composite diagram on this page.

6. Sew along the 3 straight edges. Leave the pinked edge open.

7. Insert the comb in the opening.

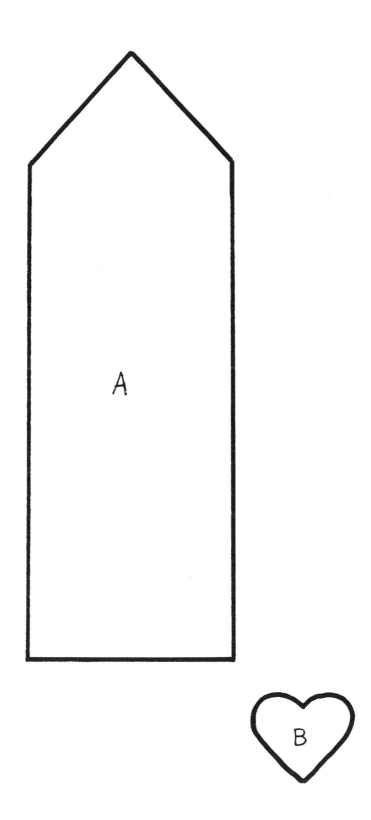

A

B

DRUM PENCIL HOLDER

materials needed

1 empty 5½-ounce juice can (any size can may be used, but
    you will have to adjust the amount of cloth needed)
1 large scrap of bright red felt measuring 3½ x 7¼ inches
1 scrap of royal blue felt

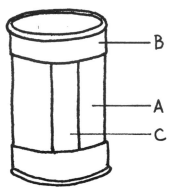

directions

Note: If the size can you use is different from the one
described here measure the height and circumference and
mark them off on the red felt, adding ¼ inch to the
circumference to allow a slight overlap. The strips marked B
and C must be adjusted in length. Pencil holder may also be
used for kitchen matches, cocktail mixers, paper clips, plastic
spoons, rubber bands, crayons, lollipops, hair clips, etc.

1. Cut out the piece of red felt (A). With pinking shears, if you
have them, cut 3 strips of royal blue felt, 2 strips (B) measuring
7¼ inches long and ½ inch wide and 3 strips (C) measuring
3½ inches long and ½ inch wide.

2. Paste the piece of red felt around the can. Put the paste—
a thin layer—on the felt, not the can. Allow to dry thoroughly.
Then paste a 7¼-inch length of blue felt around the top of the
can and another around the bottom.

3. Now paste 1 short length of blue felt down the seam (where
the 2 ends of red felt meet). Paste the other two strips of blue
felt from top to bottom—evenly spaced—to give the design a
drum effect. Fill with pencils.

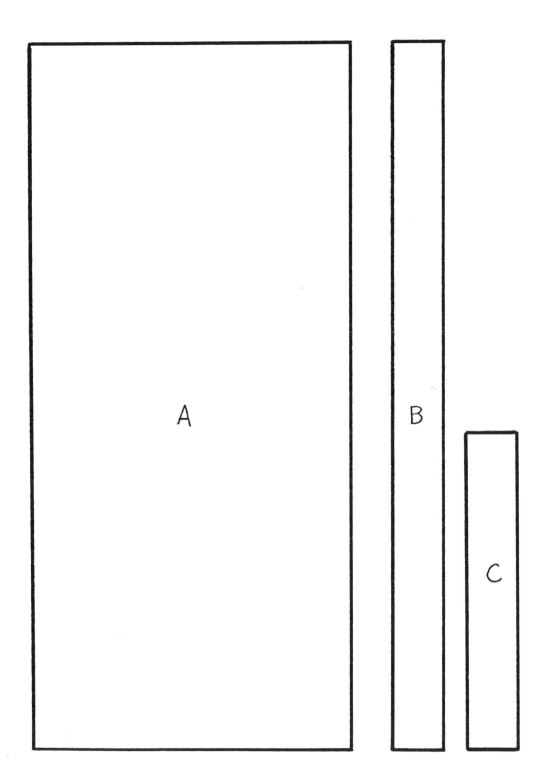

DRIED-FLOWER VASE

materials needed

1 empty 5½-ounce juice can
1 large scrap of royal blue felt (dark-colored felt works better on the cans than lighter shades) measuring 3½ x 7¼ inches (see pattern on page 111)
1 piece of matching, decorative ribbon, measuring 18 x ½ inch
12 ¼-inch sequins in assorted colors

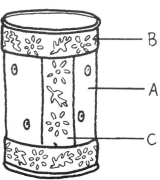

directions

1. Cut out the piece of royal blue felt (A). Cut the ribbon into 3 lengths—2 strips (B) measuring 7½ inches long and 1 strip (C) measuring 3½ inches long.

2. Paste the piece of royal blue felt around the can. Put the paste on the felt, not the can. Allow to dry thoroughly.

3. When dry, paste the shorter length of ribbon down the "seam" of the felt-covered can (this gives it a more finished look). Paste a 7½-inch length of ribbon around the top of the felt-covered can and the other around the bottom, as shown in the composite diagram on this page. Use the extra ½ inch on each piece of ribbon to tuck under so that ribbon will not unravel (or you can pink the edges and paste flat).

4. Paste the sequins in a scattered pattern around the blue felt, not on the ribbon. See diagram.

5. Fill the can with colorful dried flowers.

GLOVE OR HANDKERCHIEF CASE

materials needed

1 piece of green felt 9 x 12 inches
1 scrap of red felt
   red thread to match

directions

1. Pink the 4 edges of the green felt.

2. Turn one end up to form a 4½-inch-deep pocket, which leaves a 3-inch flap.

3. Pin the 2 sides of the pocket together.

4. With red thread, sew the sides together and continue stitching along the side of the flap, across the top of the flap, and down the other side, closing the second side of the pocket.

5. Trace the heart outline (B) on the red felt.

6. Cut out 3 red hearts.

7. Paste 1 heart on the lower right-hand corner of the case, as shown in the composite diagram on this page. Turn the flap down so that it forms an envelope, and paste 2 hearts on the outside of the flap, as shown.

8. Fill with gloves or handkerchiefs.

APPLE PINCUSHION

materials needed

1 piece of red felt for the apple (makes 2 pincushions)
1 scrap of green felt for the stem
1 scrap of white felt for 4 ¼-inch dots
   red thread to match
   cotton for stuffing (use inexpensive hospital cotton)

directions

Note: All pincushions may be stuffed with beans instead of cotton and used as beanbags.

1. Fold the piece of red felt in half and cut into 2 equal parts.

2. Trace the apple (A) on the red felt. Trace the stem (B) on the green felt.

3. Cut out 2 apple parts. Cut out 1 green stem. Cut or punch out 4 white ¼-inch dots.

4. Paste or pin the green stem between the 2 apple parts at the top, as shown in the composite diagram on this page. Paste the 4 white dots on the front of the apple, as shown. Allow to dry.

5. Pin the 2 apple sides together (stem should be between the 2 apple parts).

6. Sew the pincushion all around, but leave a 3-inch opening.

7. Stuff enough cotton into the opening so that you can put a pin all the way into the cushion without its coming through the other side. But don't overstuff it.

8. Finish the pincushion by sewing up the opening and removing pins.

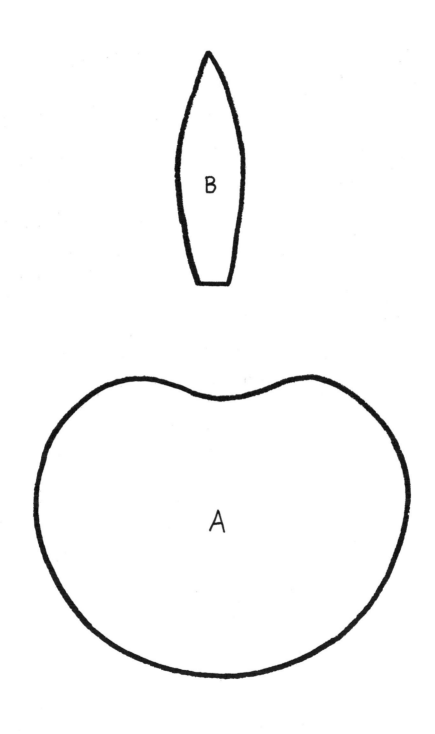

PEAR PINCUSHION

materials needed

1 piece of yellow felt for the pear (makes 2 pincushions)
1 scrap of green felt for the stem
1 scrap of brown felt for 4 ¼-inch dots
   yellow thread to match
   cotton for stuffing

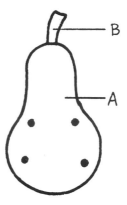

directions

Note: All pincushions may be stuffed with beans instead of cotton and used as beanbags.

1. Fold the piece of yellow felt in half and cut into 2 equal parts.

2. Trace the pear (A) on the yellow felt. Trace the stem (B) on the green felt.

3. Cut out 2 yellow felt pear parts. Cut out 1 green stem. Cut or punch out 4 brown ¼-inch dots.

4. Paste or pin the green stem between the 2 pear parts at the top, as shown in the composite diagram on this page. Paste the 4 dots on the front of the pear, as shown. Allow to dry.

5. Pin the 2 pear sides together.

6. Sew the pincushion all around, but leave a 3-inch opening.

7. Stuff enough cotton into the opening so that you can put a pin all the way into the cushion without its coming through the other side.

8. Finish the pincushion by sewing up the opening and removing pins.

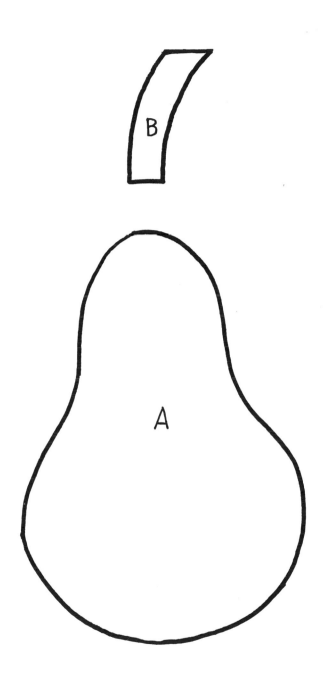

B

A

STRAWBERRY PINCUSHION

materials needed

1 piece of red felt for the strawberry (makes 2 pincushions)
1 scrap of green felt for the stem
1 scrap of black felt for 6 ¼-inch dots
   red thread to match
   cotton for stuffing

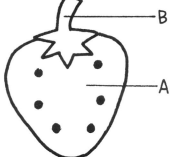

directions

Note: All pincushions may be stuffed with beans instead of cotton and used as beanbags.

1. Fold the piece of red felt in half and cut into 2 equal parts.

2. Trace the strawberry (A) on the red felt. Trace the stem (B) on the green felt.

3. Cut out 2 red felt strawberry parts. Cut out 1 green stem. Cut or punch out 6 black ¼-inch dots.

4. Paste the 6 black dots in place, as shown in the composite diagram on this page.

5. Pin the 2 sides of the pincushion together.

6. Sew the pincushion all around, but leave a 3-inch opening.

7. Stuff enough cotton into the opening so that you can put a pin all the way into the cushion without its coming through the other side.

8. Sew up the opening and cut off any loose ends of thread.

9. Now, paste the stem at the top of the strawberry (on the outside), as shown.

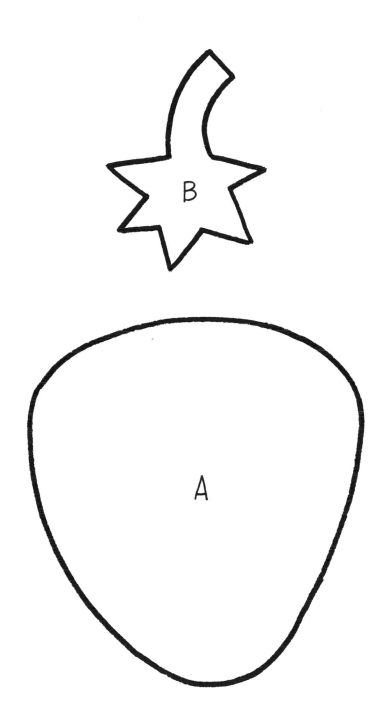

PUMPKIN PINCUSHION

materials needed

1 piece of orange felt for the pumpkin (makes 2 pincushions)
1 scrap of green felt for the stem
1 scrap of brown felt for 6 ¼-inch dots
   orange thread to match
   cotton for stuffing

directions

Note: Decorate for Hallowe'en by using 3 black ½-inch triangles for the eyes and nose and a black, smiling mouth. Omit the brown dots. Stuffed with beans instead of cotton, this pincushion becomes a beanbag.

1. Fold the piece of orange felt in half and cut into 2 equal parts.

2. Trace the pumpkin (A) on the orange felt. Trace the stem (B) on the green felt.

3. Cut out 2 orange pumpkin parts. Cut out 1 green stem. Cut or punch out 6 brown ¼-inch dots.

4. Paste the stem between the 2 pumpkin parts at the top, as shown in the composite diagram on this page. Paste the six dots on the pumpkin, as shown. Allow to dry.

5. Sew the pincushion all around, but leave a 3-inch opening.

6. Stuff enough cotton into the opening so that you can put a pin all the way into the cushion without its coming through the other side.

7. Finish the pincushion by sewing up the opening.

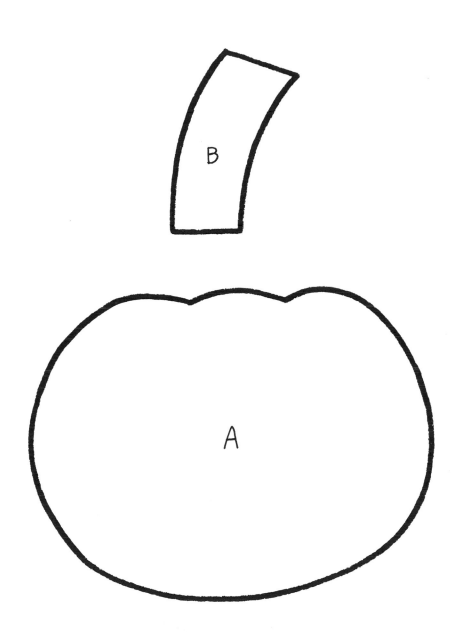

DOLL'S TUNIC

materials needed

2 pieces of orange felt (makes 2 tunics)
1 scrap each of white, black, and red felt

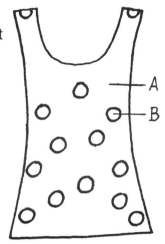

directions

1. Trace the outline of the tunic (A) on the orange felt. Trace the outline of the circle on the white, black, and red felt.

2. Cut out 2 orange tunic patterns. Cut out 12 black circles, 10 white circles, and 6 red circles.

3. Pin the 2 sides together.

4. Paste 12 colored circles on the front of the dress, as shown in the composite diagram on this page. Mix up the colors. Paste 12 more colored circles on the back of the dress in the same way.

5. Put a dab of glue on the shoulder straps of the back part. Cover about ½ inch of felt with glue. Press the 2 front shoulder straps over the 2 back ends to join them. They should overlap about ½ inch.

6. Paste a black circle on 1 shoulder to cover seam. Paste a white circle on the other shoulder.

7. Hang the tunic on a doll's hanger.

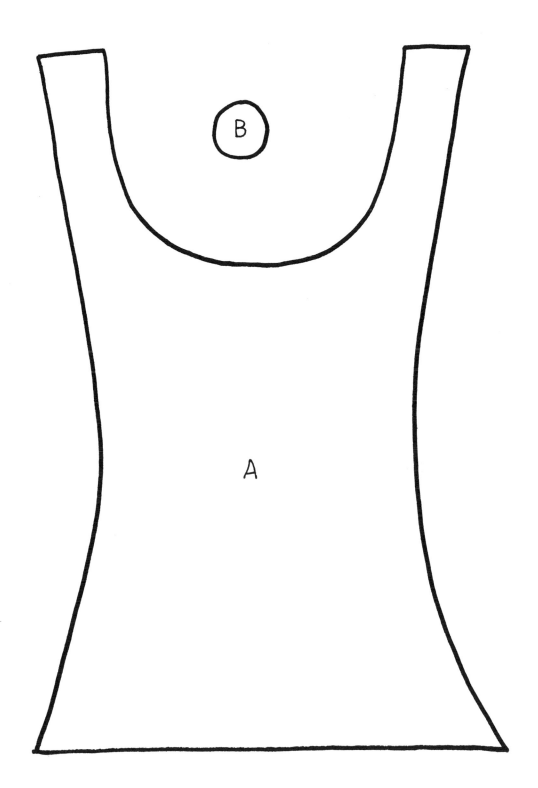

DOLL'S DRESS

materials needed

2 pieces of pink felt (makes 2 dresses)
1 scrap of red felt for the heart decorations
   small ¼-inch colored sequins

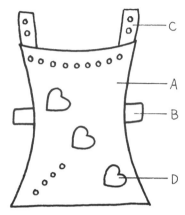

directions

1. Trace the dress (A) on pink felt. Trace the shoulder straps (C) and side bands (B) on pink felt. Trace the hearts on red felt.

2. Cut out 2 pink dress patterns with pinking shears. Cut out 2 pink shoulder straps and cut only the curved side with pinking shears, if available, the other with straight scissors. Cut out 2 pink side bands with straight scissors. Cut out 3 red hearts.

3. Paste the hearts and sequins on the front of the dress, as shown in the composite diagram on this page. Paste the sequins on the shoulder straps, as shown.

4. Put a dab of glue on the 2 ends of 1 side band, covering about ½ inch of felt, and press each end on the inside of the front and back of the dress. Side band should be in the middle of the dress where the waist is curved. Repeat for the other side band, matching them up perfectly.

5. Do the same for the shoulder straps, pressing each glue-covered ½ inch of strap to the inside of each shoulder of the dress. Line up the pinked edge of the shoulder straps with the pinked edge of the dress.

6. Hang the dress on a doll's hanger.

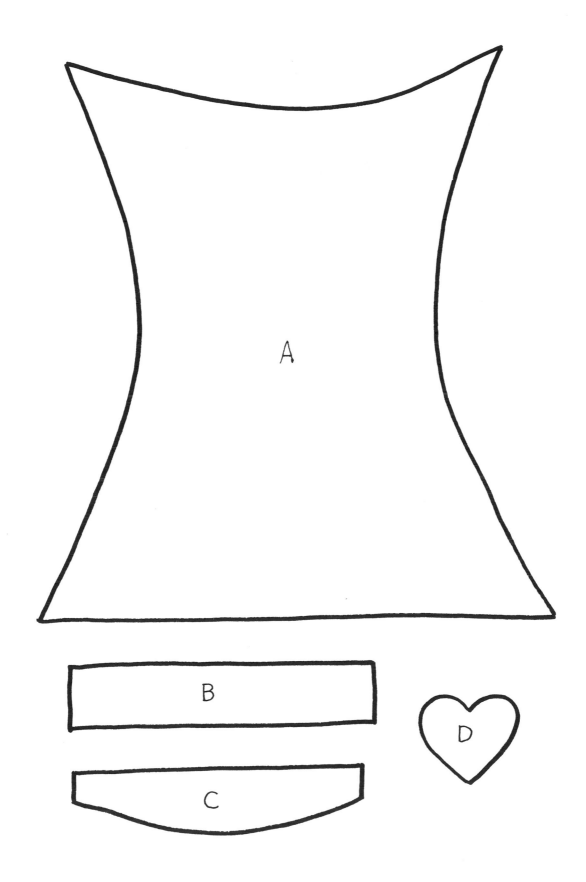

8. a word to the wise: don't!

In the introduction, I stated that no matter how successful your felt items are, you should think twice—and then twice again—about going into business and trying to mass-produce them. Unfortunately, I just thought once when someone said to me, "Why don't you go into business and *sell* these great-looking gifts?" It started two months after I had made the gifts for Christmas.

One day, I wandered into a neighborhood gift shop owned by a friend of mine. I needed a birthday gift for a niece. Modestly, I said to my friend, "Sue, I made gifts this past Christmas that are cuter than some of the things you have here."

"Let's see them," she said. So I showed her some examples of my work a few days later.

Sue looked at them for a minute. Then she said, "Make me a dozen chicken beanbags, a dozen ladybug beanbags, and a dozen frog beanbags."

And suddenly, I was in business.

There I was with my first order and a few mangy felt scraps in my closet. Obviously, if I was to make money, I had to purchase my supplies at wholesale prices. But where does one buy felt wholesale? And beans? And thread?

For years I had read and heard that clever little jingle, "Let your fingers do the walking through the yellow pages." So, sitting cross-legged on my bed with Mr. Bell's handy little invention beside me, I walked, danced, and ran through the yellow pages from AAAA to ZZZZ. Starting with FELT, I finally discovered under C a company that would sell me a quantity less than 100,000 yards. It took me all the way to S to find a glue company that would condescend to let go of a little less than 400 cartons, *packed 24 containers to the carton.* But under FOOD, I couldn't find a single bean company. And A & P won't tell.

Then I bought an order book and an account book and totted up my expenses. It was rather a shock to find that my supplies had cost me $3.75 more than my first order would bring in.

"This is ridiculous," I said to myself. "Here I am with one tiny order and a large array of felt lying fallow after this order is filled. I'll face reality! I'll go to B. Altman, F. A. O. Schwarz, and Saks Fifth Avenue and see what *they* think."

So I made a little trip to see the buyer at B. Altman & Co.

He came out rubbing his forehead. Being a great believer in omens, I thought: Great, my first big-time buyer and he has to have a headache. But suddenly, I was in his office with my husband's best suitcase as my sample case, nervously fumbling for the catch.

He didn't like my pajama bags, my toy bags, my marble bags, or my shoe bags. But he *loved* my beanbags.

"Okay," he said,"I'll take a gross of these—assorted."

"Fine," I tittered. "What's a gross?"

He gave me a wry smile. "Now, what are your terms, Mrs. Goldman?"

"Terms? What are terms?" I asked. Suddenly, the wry smile turned to one of disbelief.

"Mrs. Goldman, how long have you been in business?" he demanded.

My newfound confidence and exhilaration vanished. Meekly, I whispered, "One week—and you're my second customer."

My future with B. Altman & Co. lay in the balance, and finally this dear, sweet, understanding man roared with laughter.

"Sit down, Mrs. Goldman, sit down," he chuckled. For the next half hour I learned that a gross is 12 dozen; that "terms" means how payment is made for delivered merchandise; that an invoice must be sent in triplicate with each order.

When class was over, he asked me when I could deliver the beanbags. "Three weeks," I said bravely and optimistically.

The buyer gave one more roar and I wondered what I had flunked this time.

"Most people in your business say they can deliver yesterday," he told me.

At any rate, I floated out of his office and into the nearest phone booth. Getting my husband out of an important business conference, I squealed, "I did it, I did it! I sold B. Altman's a gross of beanbags."

"Great!" my husband shot back. "What's a gross?"

The next week, with the sweet smell of success luring me on, I ventured forth to F. A. O. Schwarz. By now I had developed 15 different beanbag designs.

When the buyer said she wanted 2 gross of my beanbags, I smugly whipped out my felt-covered order book and wrote:

"24 dozen beanbags: 12 frog; 12 ladybug."

By now, my dining room had begun to look like a pre-industrial revolution sweatshop. While my automatic washer-dryer hummed in the kitchen and my latest model vacuum effortlessly picked up the lint, I was laboriously cutting each of those ladybugs, frogs, and chickens by hand. But that wasn't the worst of it. Each animal had eyes, feet, mouth, nose, and various other minute parts that also had to be cut by hand and then pasted on. In desperation, I employed a new worker—my husband. Night after night, he sat next to me cutting out white noses, black eyes, and pink mouths. It was utter togetherness.

While cutting frogs one day, the phone rang. "Mrs. Goldman? This is Miss Brent of Dun & Bradstreet. I understand that you recently went into business."

I was such a neophyte and so impressed that, if you'll pardon the expression, I spilled the beans to all her questions.

"Would you mind telling me how many square feet you have in your factory?"

I looked out into my Early American, felt-covered dining room and stammered, "Well, it isn't exactly a factory, it's more like a dining room."

After a few more perfunctory questions, she asked if I'd mind telling her how much I'd invested in my business. I didn't mind.

"Do you want it in dollars and cents or just a round figure?" I asked helpfully.

"Oh, a round figure will do," she purred.

"Fifty-eight dollars," I said.

Long silence.

"Well, thank you very much, Mrs. Goldman, and"—a brief hesitation here—"and good luck to you."

I later found out, when someone tried to check, that Dun & Bradstreet did *not* give me a credit rating.

Do you think I'd rest on my laurels and let well enough alone after I finally delivered the first orders? Not me! I went out and drummed up more business. I sold dozens of shops from Greenwich Village to the upper East Side of Manhattan. Meanwhile, my friends envied me, my poor neglected children missed me, and my husband, well, in his sleep he kept muttering something about felt eyes, noses, and mouths.

I decided to play it smart with my Christmas orders. I'd get the orders in May, retire to my country house in June, and have all summer to produce them. I'd start with Saks Fifth Avenue.

This buyer, like all previous ones, was delightful to me. Yes, she'd order for Christmas, but in the meantime, how about a small "camp gift" order for the coming summer?

I had no qualms about handling a small order. The "small order" arrived in the mail the next day. I thought I'd need the F.B.I. to decode it, but when the fog finally cleared, I realized it was an order for nine branch stores and the totals, for a manufacturer of my ilk and with my production setup, were astronomical. Also, the order was due for delivery in two weeks. All I had to deliver was 24 dozen beanbags and 100 clipboards. I panicked.

After a sleepless night with felt frog legs and beady, black ladybug eyes swimming in my unconscious, I got up, determined to produce the order within the allotted two-week period. With newfound energy, I spread the felt out on the "factory table" and leafed lazily through the mail before settling down. Oh yes, I remember the day well. It was a Saturday, a balmy May morning. The balmy May morning mail contained my sixth re-order from F. A. O. Schwarz, and it *equaled the Saks order in quantity.*

I panicked! And this time, I cried. I turned to my poor, long-suffering husband and demanded through my sobs, "Why didn't you stop me? Why did you let me go on?"

"You will get those two orders out," my husband declared. "You will ship them. Then you are not to solicit any more orders. I am not punching out any more eyes. I do not want the floor carpeted with felt anymore. You are not going to neglect your family another minute. You are to give up this business here and now."

"Give it up?" I asked myself. "After all I've been through? How could I?" Then a thought struck me. I *would* give up everything—except the designing. I'd get someone else to handle the production, selling, buying, billing, and all the thousand and one headaches that go along with any business. I would design gay and unusual children's accessories and collect a royalty. A great wave of relief swept over me, and I plunged into my last two orders with enthusiasm.

On the last evening of May, everything was finished. While I packed, my husband typed invoices. It was a hot night and we had a couple of gin and tonics to celebrate the end of an era. We were getting euphoric as the end grew nigh. We giggled. We cavorted, and at 2 A.M., we tied the last cord around the last box. Then we fell into bed exhausted, but with a sigh of relief.

Connecticut welcomed me and I spent a relaxing two weeks cleaning, scouring, polishing, and weeding.

On June 15, I drove into New York to sign a contract with a manufacturer who was going to produce my designs and pay me a royalty.

I also had an appointment with the vice-president of F. A. O. Schwarz. If he chose any of my beanbags, they would appear in the Christmas catalogue. Joy unbounded! He chose three of them. At the same time, he handed me the first Christmas order to be delivered on September 1. Three gross—36 dozen—432 beanbags. I delivered the order to my manufacturer and then drove back to Connecticut with the lazy summer stretching endlessly before me.

All happy dreams and times eventually end. The summer did and the Goldmans trekked back to New York. It was then September 15. The next day the buyer from F. A. O. Schwarz called.

"Where was the September 1 order?" she asked. I called the manufacturer. It was almost finished, he said, and would be shipped by the end of the week. The message was relayed. The following week the buyer from F. A. O. Schwarz called again.

Where was the September 1 order? I phoned the manufacturer. The order was on the truck. The message was relayed.

This same conversation was repeated several more times. The only difference was that while the order was always on the truck, there was a teamster strike, a blowout, a flood, or some other disaster.

F. A. O. Schwarz wanted the beanbags for the first of October opening of its 100th anniversary Christmas Toy Bazaar. On the first of October, I began to have vague feelings of unrest. "I think I'd better go out to the factory," I told my husband. "I'll go with you," he gallantly offered.

Canceling four appointments, he drove me to the scene of the crime. Mr. Manufacturer nodded a curt acknowledgment of our presence and promptly disappeared. I went into the factory which I had visited several times before and collared the production manager. "Where are my beanbags?" I demanded hysterically. "I just finished stamping out the first dozen," he said. "The felt arrived yesterday and the beans just came this morning."

I was too stunned to panic. I simply could not believe my ears. Then my adrenalin started to flow. A sword flashed at my hip and five stars appeared on my shoulders. "You" — I shouted — "start filling those gingerbread boys! You — sew them up. You — get me boxes so I can pack them." The production manager cringed in the corner.

Three hours and fifteen minutes later, my husband and I raced to the door of F. A. O. Schwarz and delivered the first 3 dozen beanbags of the over-all order. It was 4:45 P.M. We had made it! My gingerbread boys, my Santas, and my dear little deer would be on display at the 100th anniversary Christmas Toy Bazaar.

I didn't have time to dwell on the psychotic aspects of the manufacturer's personality — nor on my own "astute" judgment in choosing him to take over my production. Now, in my hot little fist, I had an order from B. Altman & Co. for umpteen beanbags and a note from the buyer saying that one of them would appear in that store's Christmas catalogue, too. I had many other orders from my old customers. How was I going to fill them? Compared to these Christmas orders, my spring production had been a drop in the old oaken bucket.

I had three alternatives:

1. I could attempt to fill them myself, which seemed like a desperate move.

2. I could let the manufacturer attempt to do it, which seemed even more desperate.

3. I could attempt to find someone else to produce them.

Through a friend, I was introduced to the director of the National Industries for the Blind, the parent organization for many industrial groups for the blind. He put me in touch with the Jewish Guild for the Blind because its physical plant was equipped to handle my production requirements.

After many discussions and experiments, the Guild came up with some brilliant improvising so that the blind workers could make the beanbags and some of the other items.

They would "feel" the colors of the felt by the size and shape of the container which stored the pre-cut parts. Where a mouth or a nose or ears needed to be added, cardboard cutouts were devised which were placed over the felt. The blind workers could then feel the spot where the nose had to be pasted. Since each beanbag design required different amounts of beans, the workers used cups of different sizes which didn't require measuring, merely one scoopful.

And so my contract was accepted. The Guild was superb. The quality of the work was excellent, and from then on all orders and re-orders were filled with speed and perfection.

That Christmas is history. A half-ton of beans later, peace reigns again—if not on the whole world, at least in the Goldman household.

Now, in the quiet hours of the day, I design and make new gifts—*one at a time.* For I will never, *never* get involved in a business like that again.

I hope my story has convinced you *not* to listen to any voices about going into business. If you are still not convinced, then be prepared to work 19 hours a day, cope with the same problems and headaches a big business has— only you're the only one coping, neglect your family to the point where they may be ill-clothed and ill-fed; give up your social life, your weekends, skiing, tennis, and golf; threaten your health, to say nothing of your marriage.

My advice is to keep this, or *any* hobby simply what it is—a hobby. In that way, it will always remain fun.

Did I make a profit? Yes, a handsome one, I thought, until my husband pointed out one small detail. Had I payed myself a wage, I would have earned an average of 1½ cents an hour!

index